Contents

How to use this book

This guide is intended for travellers who wish to visit the most beautiful gardens of Ireland. The book is divided into four chapters covering the major regions. Each chapter comprises an introductory section with a regional map and a list of the gardens, followed by entries on each

garden. The entries are accompanied by at-a-glance information telling the reader about the garden's defining characteristics and nearby sights of interest. The guide also includes five "feature" gardens, illustrated by three-dimensional plans.

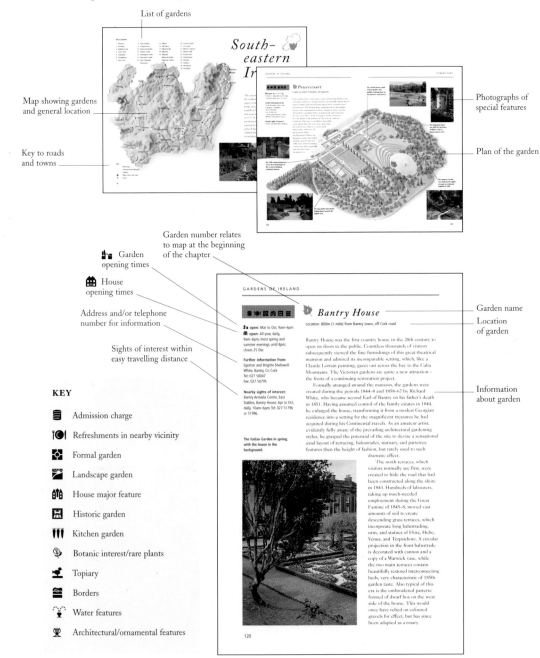

List of gardens

Map showing gardens and general location

Key to roads and towns

Photographs of special features

Plan of the garden

Garden number relates to map at the beginning of the chapter

Garden opening times

House opening times

Address and/or telephone number for information

Sights of interest within easy travelling distance

Garden name

Location of garden

Information about garden

KEY

- 🗄 Admission charge
- 🍴 Refreshments in nearby vicinity
- 🔹 Formal garden
- 🔆 Landscape garden
- ♙♙ House major feature
- 🖽 Historic garden
- 🌿🌿🌿 Kitchen garden
- 🌺 Botanic interest/rare plants
- 🌿 Topiary
- 🟰 Borders
- 🌱 Water features
- 🏺 Architectural/ornamental features

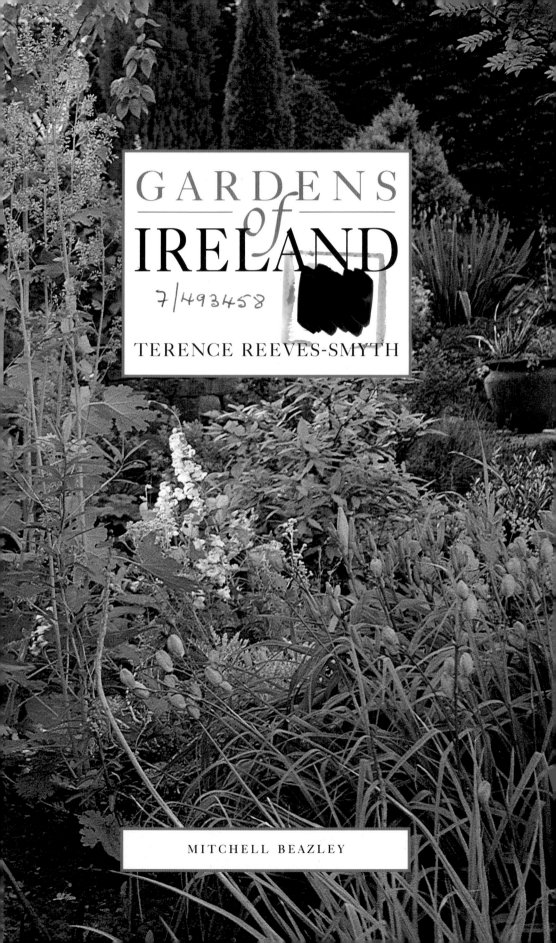

GARDENS
of
IRELAND

7/493458

TERENCE REEVES-SMYTH

MITCHELL BEAZLEY

In fond memory of Corona and Gary North

First published in 2001 by Mitchell Beazley, an imprint of
Octopus Publishing Group Ltd, 2–4 Heron Quays
London E14 4JP

A CIP record for this book is available from the British Library

ISBN 1 84000 338 3

Deputy Art Director: Vivienne Brar
Senior Editor: Michèle Byam
Executive Art Editor: Tim Brown
Designer: Terry Hirst
Editor: Selina Mumford
Contributing Editor: Richard Dawes
Production: Catherine Lay
Picture Researcher: Jenny Faithfull
Illustrator: Paul Guest
Cartographer: Kevin Jones
Indexer: Laura Hicks

Half title page: The White Garden at Lodge Park
Title page: Borders at Glebelands, Ratoath
Contents page: Box-edged paths in the walled garden at Woodville

The publisher wishes to thank all those who contributed in collating
reference material for the feature gardens.

The opening times for the gardens are correct at the time of going
to press but before travelling we strongly advise you to check with the
gardens or tourist board for the latest hours of opening.

Printed in China

Foreword

During the 1990s garden visiting outstripped golf to become the fastest-growing tourist sector in Ireland. The number of gardens open to the public continues to rise as the country's increasingly affluent and cosmopolitan society discovers the delights of gardening. New gardens are being created at a rate not seen for a century, while numerous old country-house pleasure grounds, many abandoned for generations, have reawakened from their slumber to a new and energetic life. The process has been aided by tax incentives and by the Great Gardens of Ireland Restoration Programme, an EC-backed government scheme, which since 1994 has brought 26 historic parks and gardens back to life in the Republic, many of which are included in this book. New garden marketing groups and festivals have also emerged across the country, further accelerating popular interest.

Unlike in most other European countries, the majority of gardens in Ireland open to the public are privately owned. Out of 109 included in this book, only nine are run by local councils and a further nine by Dúchas – the Heritage Service. In Northern Ireland six of the guide's gardens are owned by the National Trust, a property-owning charity with no counterpart in the Republic. This dominance by the private sector means that many gardens are open only by arrangement. Guide users should therefore ensure that they make appointments before turning up, while gardens should be treated with the same respect as if one were invited into someone's house. Cuttings should never ever be taken without permission, but visitors will always find that owners are more than obliging to those showing a real interest in their gardens.

Urns flanking steps leading down into the arboretum at Castlewellan, County Down.

Introduction

The gardens of Ireland are as diverse as the country's ever-changeable weather. There are small town gardens, great botanic collections and arboreta, grand formal schemes, country-house walled *potagers*, and all sizes of informal and naturalistic layouts. What unites them is an uninhibited vitality and exuberance, echoing the dramatic character of Ireland's landscapes, its equable climate, and the outgoing nature of its people.

As the popular image of Ireland tends to be one of constant rainfall, it is not always appreciated how suitable the country's weather is for gardening. The mild south-westerly winds and the warm, drifting waters from the Gulf of Mexico assure a mild, equable climate, which permits a far wider range of plants to be grown here than anywhere else at this latitude. The 20km (12½ miles) wide coastal region, where many of Ireland's important gardens are located, has a particularly mild climate with few frosts and the ability, given adequate shelter, to produce a wonderful range of subtropical plants.

While Ireland's gardens have evolved distinctive qualities of their own, thanks in some measure to the climate, their development over the centuries has inevitably reflected English trends. The bones of some early gardens still endure, such as the 1680s formal layout of canals, avenues, and *bosquets* at Killruddery (see p.95) – acknowledged as the best survival of its period in the British Isles. Arcadian parkscapes, characterized by clumps, belts, woodlands, and lakes, were adopted enthusiastically from the mid-18th century and remain a very visible feature of the

Many Irish gardens gain much from dramatic landscape settings such as that at Derreen on the coast of Kerry.

landscape despite the loss of so many country houses. Good examples can be visited at Belvedere (see p.49), Crom (see p.23), and Florence Court (see p.24), though sadly the finest 18th-century landscape in Ireland, at Carton, in Kildare, has recently been destroyed for golf courses and upmarket housing.

Walled gardens, usually isolated away from the house, were a standard feature of the 18th and 19th centuries. Generally they contained a regular path layout with glasshouses and functioned as places of pleasure and utility, with ornamental path borders screened from vegetables by espaliered fruit trees. Out of thousands that once existed, only a handful retaining original features have survived into the modern era, notably Woodville (see p.111), Rockfield (see p.73), and Benvarden (see p.20). A number have been adapted to make modern gardens, as at Walworth (see p.38), while an impressive number have been restored in recent years to their former 19th-century glory, as at Ballindoolin (see p.47), Strokestown Park (see

Herbaceous borders such as this at Kilquade are now standard features of Irish gardens.

Formal terraces at Curraghmore with sculptures of a wolf confronting a dog and her litter.

p.74), Lodge Park (see pp.70–1), and Kylemore Abbey (see pp.68–9).

Undoubtedly the biggest impact on both late 19th- and 20th-century Irish gardening was the concept of the naturalized or "wild" garden advocated by the Irish horticulturalist William Robinson. His philosophy of planting "perfectly hardy exotics under conditions where they will grow without further care" was universally adopted, leading to the creation of bog gardens, woodland and rhododendron gardens, mixed borders, and the massing of bulbs in grass. Nearly all of Ireland's gardens today, great and small, incorporate Robinsonian ideals, but his legacy is most obviously visible at Mount Usher (see pp.102–3), Fernhill (see pp.66–7), Rowallane (see pp.34–5), Altamont (see pp.82–3), and Derreen (see p.124).

With the decline of the country house from the 1920s, and a lack of staff, there was reliance on flowering trees and shrubs for effect, while herbaceous perennials became quite a rarity. This trend was dramatically reversed in the 1980s, the lead being taken by Jim Reynolds (Butterstream; see pp.54–5) and latterly by Helen Dillon (Dillon Garden, Dublin; see p.56), and Brian Cross (Lakemount; see p.135). Herbaceous borders are now a standard feature of Irish gardens open to the public, but having developed late they are free from the colour rules and boring predictability which for years have dogged English aesthetic values and practices. In Ireland bright colours are not regarded as "vulgar", but freely mixed in joyous abandon, creating borders overflowing with excitement and incident. But this lack of inhibition, which so echoes the Irish character, does not mean that the gardens are without principles of composition and design. As visitors will discover, Irish gardens have a wonderfully exhilarating combination of boldness, harmony, and restraint.

A cherub fountain flanked by *Ilex x altaclerensis* 'Golden King' in the yellow garden at Fairfield Lodge, County Dublin.

Key to gardens

1 Antrim Castle Gardens
2 Ardnamona
3 Ballydaheen
4 Beaulieu
5 Belfast Botanic Gardens Park
6 Benvarden
7 Brook Hall
8 Castle Ward
9 Castlewellan Castle: The National Arboretum
10 Crom Castle Demesne
11 Downhill
12 Florence Court
13 Glenveagh Castle
14 Guincho
15 Guy Wilson Daffodil Garden: Coleraine
16 Hilton Park
17 Knock Abbey
18 Lakeview
19 Leslie Hill
20 Mount Stewart
21 Redcot
22 Rowallane
23 Seaforde
24 Tully Castle
25 Walworth
26 Wilmont: Sir Thomas and Lady Dixon Park

Key

═══ Motorways

─── Principal trunk highways

(3) Gardens

● Major towns and cities

• Towns

Northern Ireland Region

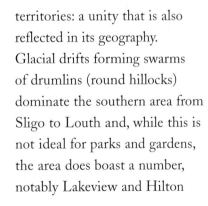

Larne

14 Bangor
A21
21 Newtownards
15 A20
Irn 20
Strangford Lough
22
A7
nahinch Portaferry
8
23 Downpatrick

Newcastle

Ireland's northern region, as defined in this book, embraces twelve counties, including all nine counties of the province of Ulster, plus Louth, Leitrim, and Sligo. The State of Northern Ireland constitutes six of Ulster's counties and forms part of the United Kingdom, whose border with the rest of Ireland (the Irish Republic) is an international boundary. There are differences in currency, road quality, and signs, among other things, so garden visitors planning cross-border routes should be prepared.

Although the region is divided politically, it shares a common history as part of Ulster and its marcher territories: a unity that is also reflected in its geography. Glacial drifts forming swarms of drumlins (round hillocks) dominate the southern area from Sligo to Louth and, while this is not ideal for parks and gardens, the area does boast a number, notably Lakeview and Hilton

**Rhododendrons and pieris provide
a backdrop to the stone herms of
Glenveagh's Italian garden.**

13

Park. The mountains occupying large parts of the region's outer rim are even less suitable, though Glenveagh famously lies in the Donegal Highlands. It is the lowland areas of east Down and north Antrim that contain many of the region's gardens, taking advantage of better soils, lower rainfall, and a milder climate.

As elsewhere in Ireland, the best gardening conditions are on the coast. Both Mount Stewart and Guincho in east Down have equable and very mild climates, where average annual rainfall is about 89cm (35in) and is balanced by high humidity, with few frosts and a growing season that lasts well into autumn. The temperate climate of these gardens allows plants to be grown from many areas of the globe, and Australasian plants are of particular importance in both. Winds can be a problem, but as in other coastal areas good shelter planting can transform a site's horticultural potential.

Mount Stewart is the region's foremost garden. It owes its survival and continuing importance to the National Trust's superb management over the past thirty years. The National Trust also owns many other gardens in Northern Ireland, notably Rowallane, whose rhododendron grounds are internationally famous. Sadly, an equivalent organization does not exist south of the border, though the Irish State plays a role through Dúchas – the Heritage Service.

In addition to gardens open regularly to the public, the Northern Ireland National Trust local garden committee organizes the opening of small private gardens at weekends from April to August. It also runs a scheme whereby many private gardens in Northern Ireland are open by appointment from May to September. Brochures for the Ulster Gardens Scheme can be obtained from: The National Trust, Rowallane, Saintfield, Ballynahinch, County Down BT24 7LH.

Lysichitons and candelabra
primulas on the lake margins
at Mount Stewart.

Antrim Castle Gardens

Location: Off Randalstown road (A6)

open: All year, daily; Mon to Fri, 9.30am–9.30pm, Sat, 10am–7pm, Sun, 2–5pm; closes 12 Jul and 25 Dec; guided tours by arrangement; teas for groups by arrangement

Further information from:
Antrim Borough Council Arts and Heritage Service, Clotworthy House, Antrim Castle Grounds, Antrim, Co Antrim BT41 4LH
Tel: 028 94428000
Fax: 028 94460360

Nearby sights of interest:
Clotworthy Arts Centre in the Castle Grounds; 10th-century round tower in the Steeple Park; Patterson's Spade Mill, Templepatrick: Apr, May and Sep, Sat, Sun and Bank Holidays, 2–6pm; Jun to Aug, daily except Tue, 2–6pm; Tel/Fax: 028 94433619 (National Trust).

Box-edged beds in the parterre.

This 15ha (37 acre) formal garden was created c1705–10 by Clotworthy Skeffington, the third Viscount Massereene, as a setting for his mansion on the north bank of the Sixmilewater River. Such geometric garden layouts went out of fashion in the 1740s with the adoption of "natural" landscaping, so when the diarist, gardener, and watercolourist Mrs Delany came here in 1758 she noted laconically that "the garden was reckoned a fine one 40 years ago – high hedges and long narrow walks". Uniquely in Ulster, the garden survived into our own era, though sadly the family house, Antrim Castle, was burnt in 1922.

Little now remains of the house, save for a tower. It lay next to a Norman motte, which was incorporated into the garden and given a spiral path to the top. To the north is the Wilderness, a woodland form of *bosquet* with dissecting paths, originally aligned on statues and other features but now gone save for an oval pond. To one side a small enclosure surrounded by tall, clipped hedges once had a parterre, while alongside the Wilderness runs a long canal whose two sections are joined by a cascade. These are edged with paths and bordered with clipped lime and hornbeam hedges 7m (23ft) high. The adjacent 0.8ha (2 acre) enclosure contains a raised terrace planted with trained hornbeam on stilts overlooking a 1993 recreation of a parterre of the early 18th century, bounded by box hedging and filled with plants of that era.

Ardnamona

Location: On W shore of Lough Eske, off road to Harvey's Point

This woodland garden lies in the shelter of the Blue Stack Mountains and has stunning views eastwards across Lough Eske. Covering about 18ha (45 acres) and surrounded by native oak woodland, it has often been compared to a Himalayan mountain slope cloaked with vast primeval rhododendrons. Many of the rhododendrons are indeed of great age, having been planted in the 1880s and 90s, when Arthur and Georgina Wallace built up their huge shrub collections here. Further plantings were added before and after World War II by Mrs West, but from the 1950s the garden went into decline and became overgrown. In 1991 it was rescued by the present owners and restoration is continuing.

Many of the older trees belong to the first 50 years of the garden, following the building of the house in the 1830s. They include coastal redwoods, Wellingtonias, Oriental spruces, a Nikko fir, and a hiba, among many fine trees. The enormous trunk sizes of some of the *Rhododendron arboreum* suggests that they may have been planted as early as the 1850s. Many of the rhododendrons, which are planted beneath the trees and along open glades, are Himalayan species, there being fine examples of *R. barbatum*, *R. thomsonii*, *R. falconeri*, *R. griffithianum*, and *R. sinogrande*. Other shrubs here include a magnificent *Pieris formosa*, also from the Himalayas, some striking *Crinodendron hookerianum* and tree-sized griselinias.

open: All year, daily, 10am–8pm, by appointment

Further information from:
Kieran and Amabel Clarke,
Ardnamona, Lough Eske, Co Donegal
Tel: 073 22650
Fax: 073 22819

Nearby sights of interest:
Donegal Castle: Jun to Oct, daily,
9.30am–6.30pm; Tel: 073 22405.

A glimpse of Lough Eske beyond the rhododendron canopy.

Ballydaheen

Location: 2.5km (1½ miles) N of turning to Portsalon Pier. Gate on right

It is surprising to find echiums happily seeding themselves in Ireland's most northerly garden, but Ballydaheen's climate is mild, as the garden is close to the sea and screened by shelter belts. Most of the 2.2ha (5½ acre) garden postdates the 1989 house and cleverly uses the sloping topography to create linked compartments, many approached through tunnels of bamboo. There are areas for herbs, vegetables, roses, herbaceous borders, and many shrubs, while around the house is a colourful, Japanese-inspired layout. The climax to a visit to this rewarding garden is the "Seven Arches": sea caves accessible by a cliff stairway.

open: 15 May to 24 Aug, daily except Sun, 10am–3pm; also open Sat of Easter weekend; unsuitable for wheelchairs; no dogs

Further information from:
Mr and Mrs Hurley, Ballydaheen,
Portsalon, Co Donegal
Tel: 074 59091

Nearby sights of interest:
Rathmullan Heritage Centre.

Beaulieu

🏠 **open:** Mar to Sep, by appointment

🏛 **open:** By appointment

Further information from:
Nesbit Waddington,
Beaulieu House, Co Louth
Tel: 041 983557

Nearby sights of interest:
The Boyne Valley and its megalithic tombs; ruins of Mellifont Abbey and Monasterboice; Millmount Museum, Drogheda: all year, Tue to Sat, 10am–6pm, Sun, 2.30–6pm; Tel: 041 33097.

Location: 3km (2 miles) from centre of Drogheda, turn left off Balbay road and follow R167 along Boyne estuary

One of the most atmospheric places in Ireland, Beaulieu, pronounced "Bewley", was built in the 1660s and is almost the only surviving Carolean country house in the country. It has an appropriately sombre classical setting, with formal terraces sweeping down to the Boyne, while its walled garden is secluded a short distance away, overlooked by the tower of the parish church, built in 1807.

The crumbling brick walls of the 0.8ha (2 acre) garden are late 17th-century and, unusually, the area is on two levels. The lower terrace is mainly devoted to the kitchen, while the upper level is entirely devoted to a stunning series of flower borders, largely created over the past 50 years by the present owner. A long, double-bordered path straddles the upper terrace, with a conservatory at one end and a Victorian summerhouse at the other. The planting, designed to look its best in summer, is a tapestry of colours and textures. It has penstemons, foxgloves, delphiniums, phloxes, hardy geraniums, and *Lobelia tupa*; there are reds of *Achillea millefolium* and *Monarda* 'Cambridge Scarlet', pinks of *Alstroemeria hookeri* and *Chrysanthemum coccineum* and purple globes of *Allium christophii*. Near the summerhouse are box-edged borders of old rose varieties, underplanted with violas and snapdragons and backed by blue-green Irish yews.

A Victorian summerhouse gazes down on the box garden, with its roses for cutting.

Belfast Botanic Gardens Park

Location: South Belfast, between Queen's University and the Ulster Museum

The Belfast Botanic Gardens were established in 1829 when the Belfast Botanic and Horticultural Society acquired a 5.5ha (14 acre) site here. The layout established over the next ten years is basically the same today, though with additional features, notably the Palm House and Tropical Ravine. For many years there were considerable financial problems in running the garden, and in 1895 it had to be sold to Belfast Corporation and was renamed the Belfast Botanic Gardens Park. At this stage the garden lost its educational and botanical function and became a municipal park.

Today the park boasts a very fine herbaceous border, a colourful rosary (1932), a rock garden (1931) and formal bedding, but the chief draw is the famed Palm House at the north end of the garden. Built by Richard Turner of Dublin, this is one of the earliest extant examples of a curvilinear glass and cast-iron glasshouse. The two wings were built in 1839–40, the east wing being used as the stove house (as it still is) and the west wing as a cooler glasshouse. The high, elliptical dome, built by Young of Edinburgh, was added in 1852. Between 1975 and 1983 the building was renovated and now houses a small but good-quality tropical plant collection. There are also brilliantly colourful displays, rarely seen nowadays, using plants such as hyacinths, tulips, daffodils, geraniums, chrysanthemums, and cinerarias.

Another major attraction is the Tropical Ravine, built in 1886–9. Divided into temperate and stove areas, the interior has a raised balcony extending around its perimeter, allowing visitors to gaze down into the sunken ravine. In 1900–2 an extension was added for the giant waterlily which still grows here. The building was restored in the early 1980s, and now houses a lush tropical mix of cycads, palms, pitcher plants, tropical vines, and tree ferns, as well as camellias and bromeliads.

open: All year, daily, 7.30am to dusk; Palm House and Tropical Ravine, Apr to Sept, Mon to Fri, 10am–12pm and 1–5pm, Sat and Sun, 2–5pm; Oct to Mar, Mon to Fri, 10am–12 noon and 1–4pm, Sat and Sun, 2–4pm; Bank Holidays as Sat and Sun; guided tour by arrangement

Further information from:
Parks Department, The Cecil Ward Building, 4–10 Linenhall Street, Belfast BT2 8BP
Tel: 028 90320202

Nearby sights of interest:
Ulster Museum; Queen's University, Belfast.

A colourful spring display brightens the conservatory.

open: Jun to Aug, daily, 2–6pm; other times by appointment

Further information from:
Mr and Mrs Hugh Montgomery,
Benvarden, Dervock, Ballymoney,
Co Antrim BT53 6NN
Tel: 028 20741331
Fax: 028 20741955

Nearby sights of interest:
Dunluce Castle, Bushmills; Tel: 028
20731938; The Giant's Causeway;
Tel: 028 20731855.

Pyrus salicifolia 'Pendula' in the
centre of a box parterre.

 ## 6 *Benvarden*

Location: 6.5km (4 miles) E of Coleraine, off B67

There are very few fully maintained old walled gardens left
in Ireland and Benvarden's is undoubtedly the best in private
hands. Gravel paths and low box hedging divide much of the
0.5ha (1½ acre) upper garden, whose curved walls support
beautifully trained fruit. A colourful double herbaceous border
runs through the garden's centre, punctuated by pergola arches
wreathed with old rose climbers. To one side and overlooked by a
glasshouse is a rose garden: a dazzling assemblage of hybrid teas
arranged around a lily pond with an urn. There are David Austin
roses to one side, a pretty sundial, and, in the adjacent block, a
large box parterre with lavender and senecio around a weeping
pear, enlivened by vivid clumps of Livingstone daisies.

The adjacent lower garden is devoted to kitchen stuff, all
beautifully ordered behind box-edged paths in true 19th-century
style. Apples, plums, and pears are trained against the walls and
on dwarf espalier supports, while the compartments are filled
with regimented rows of vegetables and soft fruit. Glasshouses
contain pot plants, tomatoes, vines, and melons.

The nearby mansion is surrounded by much ornamental
planting, both old and new, on lawns that sweep to the Bann.
An impressive cast-iron bridge of c1870 spans the river, and
to the west lies a mid-19th-century oval pond surrounded by
rhododendrons and Irish yews.

open: By appointment

Further information from:
David Gilliland, Brook Hall,
Co Londonderry
Tel: 028 71351297

Nearby sights of interest:
Grianan of Aileach stone fort;
Londonderry city walls.

 ## 7 *Brook Hall*

Location: N of Londonderry, take Culmore road (A2) and after second roundabout
pass through gates on right marked with pair of large anchors

Brook Hall has one of Ireland's best private arboretums, with
outstanding collections of trees and shrubs beautifully disposed
and maintained. Begun in 1932 by the late Commander Frank
Gilliland, the arboretum occupies about 14ha (35 acres) west and
south-west of the elegant Regency mansion, whose magnificent
parkland sweeps down to the Foyle. It has been continuously
enlarged over the years and has been catalogued by its present
owner, David Gilliland, who succeeded to the property in 1957.

The arboretum is relatively frost-free, sheltered by old
parkland oaks, beeches, chestnuts and late 19th-century conifers.
There are more than 900 varieties of trees and shrubs, including
conifers of all shapes and sizes, mixed with flowering shrubs,
pieris, cotoneasters, berberis, cherries, and acers. Many rare trees

are present, such as *Abies pindrow intermedia*, which won a Royal Horticultural Society medal in 1944. There is a wide range of beech and oak and excellent specimens of *Nyssa sylvatica*, *Podocarpus macrophyllus chinensis*, and *Azara microphylla*. Rhododendrons are a speciality, with over 100 varieties flourishing here, while camellias are housed in the walled garden, together with some magnolias and a very fine weeping beech. Nearby in a glade lies the National Collection of *Escallonia*.

Castle Ward

Location: 1.5km (1m) W of Strangford, on Downpatrick Road (A25)

The setting for one of Ireland's most famously eccentric country houses is a 324ha (800 acre) landscape park overlooking Strangford Lough. It is a superb example of 18th- and 19th-century landscaping and a place of idyllic and serene beauty.

The park incorporates residual elements of a splendid early 18th-century formal layout, best visited from the car park by the shore, close to the 16th-century tower house of the Wards. While the nearby house of c1710 has long gone, much survives of its gardens of c1720, including yew terraces, the site of a canal between two recently replanted double rows of lime and a 550m (1,800ft) canal known as the Temple Water. The scale and grandeur of the Temple Water are particularly impressive when viewed from the south-west end, where it is aligned on the much earlier Audley's Castle. On the slopes above lie the charming Lady Anne's Temple, built around 1750, which commands fabulous views to the south of the informal landscape park laid out in the 1760s for the present house.

The park was enlarged in the mid-19th century and the old flower garden close to the house was transformed into the terraced Windsor Garden. Its sunken area once held an elaborate parterre, but the colourful bedding on its terraces retains much of its Victorian layout. Symmetrically placed cordylines and a screen of Irish yews herald the adjacent pinetum, which contains collections spruces, pines and firs. A large rockery here was probably built at the end of the 19th century.

open: All year, dawn to dusk

open: Easter, 1–6pm; Apr, May, Sep, and Oct, Sat and Sun, 1–6pm; Jun to 15 Sept, daily except Thu, 1–6pm

Further information from:
Mike Gaston, The National Trust, Strangford, Downpatrick, Co Down BT30 7LS
Tel: 028 44881204
Fax: 028 44881729

Nearby sights of interest:
Exploris Sea Aquarium, Portaferry; Tel: 028 44728062; Castle Espie Wildlife Reserve; Tel: 028 44874146; Delamont Country Park; Tel: 028 44828333.

A view over the Windsor Garden, looking towards the Irish yews.

open: All year, daily, 10am to sunset

Further information from:
Forest Service, Department of
Agriculture (NI), Castlewellan,
Co Down BT31 9BU
Tel: 028 44778664
Fax: 028 44771762

Nearby sights of interest:
Mourne Mountains; Tollymore
Forest Park; Drumena Cashel;
Legananny Portal dolmen.

open: All year, daily, 10am to sunset

Further information from:
Forest Service, Department of
Agriculture (NI), Castlewellan,
Co Down BT31 9BU
Tel: 028 44778664
Fax: 028 44771762

Nearby sights of interest:
Mourne Mountains; Tollymore
Forest Park; Drumena Cashel;
Legananny Portal dolmen.

9 *Castlewellan Castle: The National Arboretum*

Location: Adjoining Castlewellan, 6.5km (4 miles) W of Newcastle

Few arboreta in the world can match Castlewellan's remarkable collection of mature trees and shrubs, and none in the British Isles boasts so many champion trees. Established in the 1870s by the fifth Earl of Annesley, it benefits from a mild coastal climate, acidic soil, and a spectacular setting, with a huge baronial castle looming over a lake and parkland in the shadow of the Mourne Mountains. The arboretum was originally confined to the walled gardens and covered about 6ha (15 acres), but since the property was acquired by the Forest Service from the Annesley family in 1967, it has been expanded to cover over 40ha (100 acres).

From the stableyard car park there is a ten-minute walk to the Annesley Garden – the two walled gardens that constitute the arboretum's hub. The Upper Garden on the west was built c1740, while the Lower Garden was added in the 1850s as a pleasure ground with terracing, pools, and an axis path linking both gardens. Some early exotics include a pair of wellingtonias

The planting around the Heron fountain is notably profuse.

(*Sequoiadendron giganteum*) planted in 1856; however, it was not until the fifth Earl's succession in 1874 that planting began in earnest and continued until his death in 1909. Within 30 years 3,000 tree and shrub species had been planted, all expertly spaced to grow into outstanding specimens. There are now 40 champion trees here, including the original drooping juniper, *Juniperus recurva* 'Castlewellan', and the golden cypress *Cupressus macrocarpa* 'Lutea', which is a parent of the garish x *Cupressocyparis leylandii* 'Castlewellan Gold'. Other giants include *Abies concolor* 'Warrezii', *Cordyline indivisa*, and *Cupressus sargentii*, while there are outstanding collections of podocarpus, silver fir, juniper, embothrium, athrotaxis, and nothofagus. An avenue of eucryphia leading up to the conservatory terrace is spectacular in late summer.

Crom Castle Demesne

Location: At end of Newtownbutler–Crom road, 5km (3 miles) W of Newtownbutler

Arguably Ireland's finest surviving "Picturesque" parkland, Crom was designed by the landscape gardener W S Gilpin in 1834–5 for John Crichton, later third Earl of Erne. The park straddles the shores of Upper Lough Erne, which meanders dreamily around its wooded islands and peninsulas, while the focus is the great neo-Elizabethan mansion built in 1831–7 by Edward Blore. The lakeside ruins of the 17th-century castle and its sham additions serve as an eye-catcher, while the adjoining battlemented terraces enclose the site of Victorian gardens and the famous pair of 400-year-old English yews, one female and one male. Other features include Gad Island tower and many ornamental buildings, all restored by the National Trust, which acquired Crom in 1987.

open: Apr to Sept, daily; Mon to Sat, 10am–6pm, Sun, 12 noon–6pm

Further information from:
John Milmore, The National Trust, Crom, Co Fermanagh
Tel: 028 66738174
Visitor Centre: 028 66738118

Nearby sights of interest:
Galoon Island gravestones; Castle Balfour, Lisnaskea, a plantation-period castle.

Downhill

Location: On Limavady road (A2), 8km (5 miles) W of Coleraine and 1.5km (1 mile) W of Castlerock

Downhill is famous for its exquisite neoclassical park buildings, but it also boasts two lakes, extensive woodlands and a gatehouse garden. The nucleus is the dramatic ruin of the house, built in 1775–87 for Frederick Hervey, Bishop of Derry and Earl of Bristol. Poised dramatically on a cliff edge to the north is the domed Mussenden Temple (1783). Other buildings include the Lion Gate (1781), the Pigeon House (1783) and the ruins of the Mausoleum, built in 1779–83 as a memorial to the Earl-Bishop's brother.

Around the Bishop's Gate and its charming Gothick gatehouse (1783), the late Jan Eccles developed an attractive flower garden. With its lawns, flowers, shrubs, rock plants, and assortment of broken statues and masonry, the garden now extends into the wooded glen beyond. Noteworthy is a bog garden, while among the many varieties of trees in the glen are sugar maples, Russian elms and Pyrenean oaks. The woods south of the road have two enormous Sitka spruces that are among the largest in Ireland.

open: All year, daily dawn to dusk; Mussenden Temple: Easter to Oct, Sat and Sun, 2–6pm; Jun and Jul, Mon to Fri, 2–6pm

Further information from:
The National Trust
Tel: 028 70848728

The small, pretty garden around the Bishop's Gate and gatehouse.

Florence Court

Location: 13km (8 miles) SW of Enniskillen, via Sligo (A4) and Swanlinbar (A32) roads

open: All year, daily, 10am–7pm (or dusk, if earlier); closes 25 Dec

open: Apr, May and Sep, Sat, Sun and Bank Holidays, 1–6pm; Good Friday to Easter Tue, daily, 1–6pm; Jun to Aug, daily except Tue, 1–6pm; last tour 5.15pm

Further information from:
Jim Chestnutt, The National Trust, Florence Court, Co Fermanagh
Tel: 028 66348249 or 66348788
e-mail: ufcest@smtp.ntrust.org.uk

Nearby sights of interest:
Marble Arch Caves; Tel: 028 66348855; Marlbank scenic loop around Lough Macrean.

The Heather House glimpsed through the planting of the pleasure ground.

Few places are more memorable than Florence Court, whose ethereal, almost bucolic golden-grey façade, built in 1750–71, shimmers like a jewel amid the splendour of romantic parkland and mountain scenery. This is the home of the Irish yew, *Taxus baccata* 'Fastigiata', discovered in the 1760s on Cuilcagh Mountain by a tenant of Lord Enniskillen. Propagation is only possible from cuttings, so this venerable tree in the woods south-east of the house is the mother of millions of upright yews throughout the world.

Other attractions include a 2ha (5 acre) walled garden north of the house, bound on two sides by ponds. A recently revitalized rose garden lies in its southern sector, with varieties such as 'White Wing' and 'Mrs Oakley Fisher' in box-edged beds, while climbing roses and clematis festoon surrounding bagatelles. To the south of the house lies a 3ha (7 acre) pleasure ground, laid down in the 1840s, with mown lawns traversed by meandering gravel paths. It has many azaleas, viburnums, dogwoods, and rhododendrons, with fine specimens of the hybrid *R.* 'Cornish Red', plus a range of maples, cherries, medlars, and magnolias, including a large *M. virginiana*. A weeping beech overhangs a stream with moisture-loving plants, while the restored Heather House offers a place of contemplation above.

Glenveagh Castle

Location: Outside Churchill, 24km (15m) NW of Letterkenny

This amazing garden is set above an eye-stopping baronial castle, which rises theatrically above the waters of Lough Veagh amid the Donegal mountains. Begun on a desolate rocky hillside in the 1870s by Mrs Adair, a rich American heiress, the garden now embraces 4.5ha (11 acres) of formal and informal areas, filled with lush vegetation and brimming with rare and tender plants. Its present appearance owes much to another American, Henry P McIlhenny, who presented the castle and gardens to the state in 1983 as the centrepiece of the 11,330ha (28,000 acre) national park that had been established here in 1975.

One of the earliest components of the garden is the pleasure ground to the north of the castle. Its large, enclosing tree rhododendrons and Scots pines help to provide a microclimate that allows tender plants to flourish, among them the tree fern *Dicksonia antarctica*, while luxuriant seas of gunneras, rodgersias, hostas, and ferns add to its tropical effect. Some plants have reached considerable size, such as a beautiful *Magnolia tripetala* and a tall *Pseudopanax crassifolius*, while the lawn edges proffer drifts of astilbes, alchemillas, primulas, agapanthus and meconopsis amid colourful maples, azaleas, and rhododendrons.

Above lies the Belgian Walk, laid down in 1915 by convalescing Belgian soldiers. Here rhododendrons, such as the white, scented 'Lady Alice Fitzwilliam', thrive, while beyond lies a formal Italian garden with antique sculpture and terracotta pots holding Ghent azaleas and hostas. The path downhill leads to the formal walled garden beside the castle, where, in addition to herbaceous borders, there is a *jardin potager*. Rows of vegetables are interwoven with fruit and flowers, such as a glorious summer display of *Dahlia* 'Matt Armour'. Box-edged paths with spiral topiary surround a Gothick orangery by Philippe Jullian at the lower end, while a flight of steps from the *potager* cross-path leads to the View Garden and the Swiss Walk, both of which offer magnificent vistas of the rugged landscape beyond the garden's confines.

open: Easter to first Sun in Nov, daily, 10am–6.30pm (Jun to Aug, Sun, until 7.30pm); closes Fri in Oct and Nov; other times by arrangement; access to gardens by official mini-coaches only

open: as above

Further information from:
Ciaran O'Keefe, Dúchas – The Heritage Service, Glenveagh National Park, Churchill, Letterkenny, Co Donegal
Tel: 074 37088, 37090 or 37262
Fax: 074 37072

Nearby sights of interest:
Glenveagh National Park, with Heritage Centre; Glebe House and Derek Hill Gallery, Gartan; Colmcille Heritage Centre, Gartan.

The castle and its gardens overlook Lough Veagh.

Guincho

Location: 13km (8 miles) from Belfast on Bangor road; take Craigdarragh road to Helen's Bay and after 400m (¼ mile) house (number 69) is on left

open: May to Sep, by appointment

Further information from:
Nick Burrowes, Gardener for Mr and Mrs Cairns, Guincho, 69 Craigdarragh Road, Helen's Bay, Co Down
Tel: 028 90486324

Nearby sights of interest:
Ulster Folk and Transport Museum at Cultra (Hollywood): Apr, May, Jun and Sep, Mon to Fri, 9.30am–5pm, Sat, 10.30am–6pm, Sun, 12 noon–6pm; Jul, Aug, Mon to Sat, 10.30am–6pm, Sun, 12 noon–6pm; Oct to Mar, Mon to Fri, 9.30am–6pm, Sat and Sun, 12.30–4.30pm; Tel: 028 90428428; Fax: 028 90428728; North Down Heritage Centre (Town Hall, Bangor Castle): Tue to Sat, 10.30am–4.30pm; Sun, 2–4.30pm; Tel: 028 91271200.

Guincho is a plantsman's garden *par excellence*, where the emphasis is on rarity rather than aesthetically pleasing displays, though it can at times be colourful. Created between 1948 and 1979 by the late Mrs Vera Mackie, this garden of 6.5ha (16 acres) embraces a river valley, woodland, shrubberies, and extensive lawns. There are intimate enclosures around the mansion, whose elegant, Portuguese-style architecture imparts a Mediterranean ambience for the garden's outstanding collection of southern-hemisphere woody plants and herbaceous perennials.

Many of the garden's plants derived from the late Talbot de Malahide's Australasian collection. Some of these lie in the shrubbery close to the house, notably a fine specimen of the Tasmanian shrub *Acradenia frankliniae*, several olearias, and a *Banksia marginata*. In the nearby paved garden, made in 1957, a *Puya alpestris* thrives, one of a small puya collection at Guincho. A paved path, passing some of the many hebe species and cultivars introduced here directly from New Zealand, leads into the pool garden flanked by banks of *Senecio* 'Sunshine'. The round garden beyond has a large *Pseudopanax crassifolius* from New Zealand, and amid bottle-brushes and tea-trees lies the original purple-leafed elder, *Sambucus nigra* 'Guincho Purple',

The pool garden, seen from the veranda.

which Mrs Mackie found growing wild in Scotland in 1957. Other plants of note in this area are the Tasmanian *Trochocarpa thymifolia* and *Senecio brunonianus*.

Shrubberies with numerous hydrangeas, rhododendrons, and collections of herbaceous plants encircle the vast expanse of lawn south of the house. These merge with the wooded valley below, where a stream is flanked by ferns, bamboos, and many tender plants, such as *Dacrydium franklinii*, *Pseudopanax arboreus*, *Agathis australis*, and *Dicksonia antarctica*. There are a large *Gevuina avellana* and many large-leafed rhododendrons, including *Rhododendron barbatum*, *R. thomsonii*, and *R. cerasinum*, the latter being one of many Kingdon Ward introductions in this remarkable garden.

Guy Wilson Daffodil Garden: Coleraine

Location: 1.5km (1 mile) N of Coleraine on the Portstewart Road (A2) at the University of Ulster, Coleraine

For more than a century Irish breeders have proved immensely successful in the number and quality of cultivars raised. As a tribute to this success, a daffodil collection has been established in the grounds of the University of Ulster at Coleraine. It is dedicated to Guy L Wilson (1885–1962) of Broughshane, County Antrim, one of the most successful of the country's breeders.

The collection occupies the site of an old quarry and has an informal setting with island beds of shrubs interplanted with daffodils and drifts in the centre. Planting began in 1971 and rapidly expanded with donations from many countries. The garden now has around 1,600 old and modern cultivars, the majority being from Irish breeders, notably J Lionel Richardson, W J Dunlop, and Tom Bloomer. The Wilson cultivars are principally represented by white daffodils, his white trumpets being especially famous. Also noteworthy are his large-cupped whites, while his small-cupped 'Chinese White' is among the most successful daffodils ever produced.

open: All year, daily; best in Apr

Further information from:
University of Ulster, Coleraine, Co Londonderry
Tel: 028 70344141

Nearby sights of interest:
Portstewart Strand; Dunluce Castle, Bushmills; Tel: 028 20731938.

Brian Duncan's *N.* 'Crenelet' in the Daffodil Garden.

 Hilton Park

Location: 5.5km (3½ miles) from Clones, on Scotstown road

From the imposing Italianate façade of Hilton Park one gazes into superb parkland: a paradise of Arcadian seclusion, with grassland dotted with clumps of noble trees, sweeping lakes, and tree-lined glades. The house, with its attenuated Ionic portico, dates from 1872–5 and encases an 18th-century block, itself rebuilt after a fire in 1803. In 1870 Ninian Niven designed the recently restored formal parterre below the house windows and the nearby rose garden. The glasshouse site here is now a herbaceous border, while behind lies a herb garden. The grounds offer a number of lovely walks.

open: By appointment

Further information from:
Mr and Mrs Madden, Hilton Park, Scotshouse, Co Monaghan
Tel: 047 56007

Nearby sights of interest:
Monaghan County Museum, Monaghan: all year, Tue to Sat, 11am–5pm (closes for lunch 1–2pm); Tel: 047 82928.

open: May to Sep, daily
except Mon, 12 noon to 5pm;
open Mon Bank Holidays

Further information from:
Knock Abbey Castle, Ardee,
Co Louth
Tel: 042 9370690

Nearby sights of interest:
Louth County Museum, Dundalk:
Mon to Sat, 10.30am–5.30pm, Sun
and Bank Holidays, 2–6pm.

 # Knock Abbey Castle

Location: Turn right off Londonderry road (N2), 3km (2 miles) N of Ardee

The castle is composed of buildings of different periods: chiefly a 15th-century tower house, a Georgian wing, and a Regency Gothic wing. The 2ha (5 acre) gardens, reinstated to their formative 1860s phase, incorporate features for a 1730s formal layout, notably a pair of canals, adapted as a Victorian naturalistic "water garden". Restored features include a herbaceous border, shrubberies, and a hothouse, flanked by extensive rockeries and flower garden within a yew hedge. There are pleasant walks around idyllic parkland.

open: May to Sep, Thu to Sat,
2–6pm; other times by
appointment

Further information from:
Daphne and Jonathan Shackleton,
Lakeview, Mullagh, Co Cavan
Tel: 046 42480
Fax; 046 42406
e-mail: jshack@indigo.ie

Nearby sights of interest:
St Killian's Heritage Centre,
Mullagh: all year, Mon to Fri,
10am–6pm; Easter and Oct,
12.30–6pm; Tel: 046 42433.

 # Lakeview

Location: 2km (1¼ miles) W of Mullagh. Take Virginia road from Mullagh, then take first left after Mullagh Lake. Entrance 300m (330 yards) on right

The sloping terraces of Lakeview's walled garden sit snugly above the old rambling house, giving tantalizing glimpses through the trees of Mullagh Lake below. For years the garden lay derelict, but after Daphne Shackleton inherited the property in 1996 from the last of the Mortimers, owners since the 17th century, she and her husband Jonathan have transformed the

**The main herbaceous border and
rustic pergolas.**

garden into a place of seductive charm, overflowing with rare and unusual plants, many originating from the famous Shackleton garden at Beech Park near Dublin.

From the house a series of shallow terraces leads up steps into the 0.4ha (1 acre) walled garden. Divided by gravel paths and old espaliered apples, this has areas for fruit and vegetables behind herbaceous borders running down the centre. A mulberry stands guard over one ornamental vegetable bed with bands of chives flanking the path, while other plots include many globe artichoke varieties. The array of colours is dazzling: phloxes, astilbes, ligularias, agapanthus, penstemons, salvias, tradescantias, and nepetas fill the borders, with ornamental grasses such as *Stipa* and *Arundo*. There is a sparkling display of blue poppies, notably *Meconopsis* x *sheldonii* 'Slieve Donard', celmisias, including 'David Shackleton', and the double-flowering nasturtium 'Margaret Long'. A magnificent old *Magnolia soulangiana* thrives here, while a wildflower meadow and shrubberies lie below the house.

19 *Leslie Hill*

Location: From Ballymoney, take Coleraine and Newbridge road, turn left onto Macfin Road and gates are 90m (100 yards) on left

The grandest mid-Georgian house of north Antrim, Leslie Hill was started in 1755 and was still unfinished when Mrs Delany visited in 1758. To its rear lie some excellent 18th-century farm buildings, all open to the public, while the landscape park to the north, which probably dates to the 1760s, has some very fine mature trees and woodlands. These remain largely unaltered save for a lake with an island, added in the later 19th century.

The path to the walled garden, east of the house and reached through a pleasure ground, is lined with ornamental trees and shrubs. The garden, a long, narrow area of 0.5ha (1¼ acres) dating to the 1750s, was reclaimed from the wilderness during the 1990s and is currently being restored. On its west side a large lawn, formerly an elaborate box garden focused on an old melon pit, is fringed by colourful mixed borders against the walls. A central path, bordered with perennials and shrubs, leads to a herb garden and nearby are the foundations of glasshouses with fascinating hot-air flues.

open: Easter to end Jun and Sep, Sat, Sun and Bank Holidays, 2–6pm; Jul and Aug, Tue to Sat and Bank Holidays, 11am–6pm, Sun, 2–6pm; no dogs
open: Not open to visitors

Further information from:
James and Elizabeth Leslie, Leslie Hill, Ballymoney, Co Antrim
BT53 6QL
Tel: 028 27663109

The pergola in the walled garden.

20 *Mount Stewart*

Location: On Portaferry road (A20), 8km (5m) SE of Newtownards

open: Mar, Sun, 2–5pm; Apr to Sep, daily, 11am–6pm; Oct, Sat and Sun, 11am–6pm; Temple of the Winds: Apr to Oct, Sat and Sun, 2–5pm; other times by appointment

open: Apr and Oct, Sat, Sun and Bank Holidays, 1–6pm; May to Sep, daily except Tue, 1–6pm

Further information from:
Harry Hutchman, The National Trust, Newtownards, Co Down BT22 2AD
Tel: 028 42788387 or 42788487
Fax: 028 42788569
e-mail: umsest@smtp.ntrust-org.uk
Tea room: Tel: 028 42788801
Shop: Tel: 028 42788878

Nearby sights of interest:
Grey Abbey ruins and medieval physic garden: Apr to Sep, Tue to Sat, 10am–7pm, Sun, 2–7pm; closes Mon; Tel: 028 42788585.

The slopes below Tir-ña-nOg, threaded with steps, contain numerous tender and uncommon plants from around the world.

Mount Stewart is Ireland's premier garden and one of Europe's great horticultural creations. Recently nominated for World Heritage status, it is noteworthy above all for the remarkable scope of its plant collections and the originality and idiosyncrasy of its design. Created within an old demesne on the shores of Strangford Lough, the 17ha (78 acre) garden is protected by fine parkland trees planted in the 1780s. The celebrated ornamental Temple of the Winds was added to the park in 1782–3, and the house was enlarged in 1804 and in the 1830s.

The glorious colours of rhododendrons mixed with rare trees and shrubs are reflected in the shimmering waters of the lake.

There are superb views of Strangford Lough from the Temple of the Winds, built in 1782–3 by James Stuart.

The arcaded cypress hedges of the Spanish Garden, viewed from across the parterres of the Italian Garden.

31

The Shamrock Garden's yew harp.

A pig, one of the satirical animal statues in the Dodo Terrace.

Edith, Marchioness of Londonderry, created the garden from 1921. Advice was sought from eminent plantsmen, and plants were obtained from around the world that that would flourish in Mount Stewart's mild climate. Edith favoured Australasian plants and 80 per cent of her plantings are species rather than cultivars or hybrids.

The formal gardens flanking the house were designed as an extension to the grand reception rooms. The south front overlooks the parterre area known as the Italian Garden, whose simple, geometric layout has a wonderfully rich selection of herbaceous plants in beds edged with purple *Berberis thunbergii*, bronze *Thuja* 'Rheingold', *Hebe albicans*, and white *Erica erigena*. Below lies the Spanish Garden, which is noted for its loggia on an axis with the house and its arches of clipped x *Cupressocyparis leylandii*, embracing a scheme of salmon and pale-yellow flowers with grey foliage plants. A touch of humour is added by the Dodo Terrace of 1925, whose statuary beasts represent people in the high politics of the era. Beyond lies the Mairi Garden, laid out in the same year, whose beds make up the shape of a Tudor rose in a white and blue colour scheme. The colours orange, yellow, and blue dominate the Sunk Garden, designed by Gertrude Jekyll, which lies to the west of the house.

Here the scented hybrid *Rhododendron* 'Coccineum Speciosum' and *Acer* 'Crimson King' are most striking, while the enclosing pergola supports many roses; others may be found on the terrace, among them 'Lord Castlereagh' and *R. gigantea*.

The Mairi Garden, looking towards the summerhouse.

The Shamrock Garden, which incorporates a good deal of topiary, leads into the informal parts of the garden, where paths wind through shrubs and woodland, all elegantly and cleverly planted. The most important plants here are undoubtedly eucalyptus (Mount Stewart's tree screens are so effective that the garden supports one of the best collections of eucalyptus in the British Isles), metrosideros, phyllocladus, pittosporum, leptospermum, cordyline, and sophora from Australasia, and luma and embothrium from South America. A focal point of the Shamrock Garden is the lake, created in the 1840s, the perimeter of which was richly planted by Lady Londonderry with masses of colourful flowering trees and shrubs. Above, on a south-facing hill, stands the family burial ground, Tir-ña-nOg, which offers glorious views of the garden and Strangford Lough.

33

open: May to Sep, by appointment

Further information from:
Mr Knox Gass in Belfast
Tel: 028 90796614

 ## Redcot

Location: From Upper Newtownards Road, turn right at Knock lights onto Knock road, then take second right onto King's Road (house number 35, on left)

Redcot's 1ha (2½ acre) garden presents an outstanding collection of shrubs and perennials in a well-designed setting that somehow feels far from town, even though it lies in the heart of Belfast's suburbs. Surrounding a Tudor-style house of the 1880s, it encompasses quite different areas, but plants are allowed to seed themselves throughout in classic Robinsonian style.

Elements of the Victorian planting survive in the front, where a beautiful *Cedrus deodara* dominates the lawn. Here are an old *Sequoiadendron giganteum* and *Arbutus unedo*, while the sandy soil, quite different from the rest of the garden, allows good magnolias,

View from the back lawn towards the house.

notably a floriferous *Magnolia* x *proctoriana*. The house rear is flanked by a lawn, laid down in the 1980s, fringed by mixed borders, while wisteria and the vigorous white *Rosa filipes* 'Kiftsgate' cloak the building. On one side is a magnificent 30m (100ft) herbaceous border backed by yew hedging and on the other a glasshouse and propagating area. In the shade of beech trees below are collections of ferns (over 100 varieties) and hellebores, while the "low garden" beyond has moisture-loving plants such as gunneras and a fine mix of self-seeding irises, meconopsis, orchids, primulas, and echiums amid camellias, hydrangeas, and other ornamental shrubs.

open: Apr to Oct, Mon to Fri, 10.30am–6pm, Sat and Sun, 2–6pm; Nov to Mar, Mon to Fri, 10.30am–5pm; closes 25–6 Dec and 1 Jan

Further information from:
The Head Gardener, The National Trust, Rowallane, Saintfield, Ballynahinch, Co Down BT24 7LH
Tel: 028 97510131

Nearby sights of interest:
Legananny Portal dolmen.

 ## Rowallane

Location: 800m (½ mile) S of Saintfield, on Downpatrick road (A7)

Rowallane is renowned for spectacular spring-colour displays, especially of rhododendrons and azaleas, which are skilfully and boldly integrated into the undulating topography of the 21ha (52 acre) site. The garden has an extensive collection of summer-flowering plants and also features wildflower meadows, a rock garden, and a fine tree collection.

Although the garden's horticultural importance was chiefly due to Hugh Armytage Moore, it was his uncle, the Reverend John Moore, who laid the groundwork, from 1861. He transformed a barren hillside into a wooded parkland and built the idiosyncratic stone seats and cairns along the main avenue. Hugh Armytage Moore developed his inheritance from 1903, using many of the novel plants of the day. He raised many plants from seed collected by plant hunters, notably Ernest Wilson, George Forrest, and Francis (Frank) Kingdon Ward, and developed a number of his own hybrids. In 1955 the National Trust took over the gardens, and thanks to the high quality of its staff Rowallane remains a garden of enormous importance.

Some of the most interesting plants lie in the walled garden adjacent to the house. Here may be found a great display of meconopsis, notably *Meconopsis* x *sheldonii* 'Slieve Donard', and there are collections of primulas, including the vigorous 'Rowallane Rose', the National Collection of *Penstemon*, and the distinctive *Crocosmia masoniorum* 'Rowallane'. The early-flowering *Viburnum plicatum tomentosum* 'Rowallane' is here, and in the outer enclosure is the first *Magnolia dawsoniana* ever to flower in the British Isles. Here also is a collection of hydrangeas, notably the large *Hydrangea sargentiana*, the original crimson *Chaenomeles* x *superba* 'Rowallane', and the famous yellow-cupped *Hypericum* 'Rowallane' hybrid.

The garden's succession of enclosures contain superb specimens of *Oxydendrum arboreum*, *Davidia involucrata*, *Acer forrestii*, *Styrax japonicus*, *Desfontainia spinosa*, and a huge *Pterocarya fraxinifolia*. There is a major collection of *Nothofagus*, while everywhere are massed plantations of rhododendrons and azaleas, enlivened with berberis, viburnums, Himalayan magnolias, and sorbus.

Great banks of rhododendrons in the Spring Ground.

35

 ### 23 *Seaforde*

Location: On Newcastle road (A24), N of Seaforde

open: Mar to Oct, Mon to
Sat, 10am–5pm, Sun, 1–6pm; Nov
to Feb, Mon to Fri, 10am–5pm;
closes 25 Dec to 1 Jan

Further information from:
Patrick Forde, Seaforde House,
Seaforde BT30 8PG
Tel: 028 44811225
Fax: 028 44811370

Nearby sights of interest:
Clough Motte and Castle;
Maghera Church and Round
Tower; Ballynoe Stone Circle.

In the 1970s Patrick and Lady Anthea Forde created a new garden on the site of a derelict Victorian ornamental garden on the edge of Seaforde demesne. In the centre of this 0.8ha (2 acre) walled garden they planted a hornbeam maze enclosing a rampant *Rosa longicuspis*. Several sophora and a colony of self-seeding echiums now occupy the area of the old glasshouses to the north, while further along lies a mogul-like tower to allow visitors to admire the maze. Alongside this are avenues of shrubs containing hydrangeas, lilies, *Melianthus major*, and a number of azaras, including *Azara microphyllia* and *A. serrata*. Here too is the National Collection of *Eucryphia*; there are currently 19 cultivars of these fragrant white-flowering southern-hemisphere plants.

South of the walled garden lies a secluded, undulating, grassy area known as the Pheasantry. Of note here is an enormous *Rhododendron arboreum*, a magnificent Crimean pine, *Pinus nigra caramanica*, and at least eleven varieties of azara planted in the shade of the trees. A small pond is surrounded by moisture-loving plants with drifts of summer-flowering camassias in the shade.

The Butterfly House in the nursery end of the garden contains a selection of tropical plants. These include no fewer than three varieties of *Dicksonia* and *Cyathea*, a Brazilian spider-flower, *Tibouchina semidecandra*, daturas, and banana plants.

The hornbeam maze, seen from the mogul-style tower.

Tully Castle

Location: 5km (3 miles) N of Derrygonnelly, at end of lane off Belleek road (A46)

This stronghouse and bawn, built in 1612–15, was gutted and abandoned in the 1641 rebellion after it was surrendered to Rory Maguire, and the occupants, 16 men and 69 women and children, were massacred. During repair of the building in the 1970s, excavation revealed the bawn to be divided by cobbled paths, which in 1988 formed the basis of a garden reconstruction.

The planting was designed to reflect the appearance of early 17th-century gardens as they may have been at that time. Compartments of box, all subdivided, were filled with plants known to have been available during the period, which include pot marigolds, wallflowers, viola tricolors, roses, southernwood, sweet bay, lavender, and hyssop. Native herbs include lovage, tansy, lemon balm, sweet Cicely, and marjoram.

open: Apr to Sep, Tue to Sat, 10am–7pm, Sun, 2–7pm

Further information from:
Environment and Heritage Service, 5–33 Hill Street, Belfast BT12LA
Tel: 028 90543037 or 90543033
Website: www.ehsni.gov.uk

Nearby sights of interest:
ExplorErne (Corry, Belleek) exhibition: 14 Mar to 3 Nov, daily, 10am–6pm; Tel: 028 68658866; Monea Castle; Boho High Cross; Boa Island stone figures.

Part of the bawn garden.

25 *Walworth*

Location: 1.5km (1 mile) NW of Ballykelly

open: By appointment to groups

Further information from:
Noreen and Brian Brown,
Walworth Gardens, Ballykelly,
Limavady, Co Londonderry BT49 9JU
Tel: 028 77762671

Nearby sights of interest:
Roe Valley Country Park.

A trellis bower and seat at one end of the garden.

Walworth's walled garden is probably contemporary with the 1740s manor, though it lies adjacent to the remains of a plantation bawn built by the Fishmongers' Company from 1609. The 0.4ha (1 acre) enclosure, separated from the manor by lawns and trees, once served as a kitchen garden, but from 1989 has been redesigned as a magnificent ornamental garden.

The garden's formal path network is retained, as are the perimeter gravel paths edged with vigorous alpines, such as *Phlox douglasii* 'Red Admiral' and *Pratia pedunculata*. The wall-side borders are filled with perennials such as astrantias, campanulas, and hostas, mixed with shrubs, notably roses, with pyracanthas and climbing hydrangeas behind. Lawns and shrub beds dominate the main area, with brick paths meeting at a central pool, enclosed by a pergola festooned with clematis, wisteria, kolomikta vines, and roses. Massed floribunda and hybrid tea roses occupy beds outside the pergola, while a mixture of lavender, dianthus, green hebes, and phlomis hide the rose stems in front. More roses grow on trellis arches and pyramids in what is very much a summer garden.

26 *Wilmont: Sir Thomas and Lady Dixon Park*

open: All year, daily; walled garden: Mon–Fri, 8am–4pm, weekends, 2–4pm

Location: 2.5km (1½ miles) SE of Dunmurry on Upper Malone Road, S of Belfast

Further information from:
Belfast City Council, Parks
Department, The Cecil Ward
Building, 4–10 Linenhall Street,
Belfast BT2 8BP
Tel: 028 90320202

Nearby sights of interest:
Barnett Demesne and Malone
House; Tel: 028 90681246.

Covering 52ha (128 acres) on the east bank of the River Lagan, Wilmont is an attractive 19th-century landscape park, now municipally owned and best known as the home of the City of Belfast International Rose Garden, one of the world's largest and most spectacular rose collections. In 2000 it was given a plaque of merit, a rare honour, by the World Federation of Rose Societies.

An international rose trials ground was initially set up here with government backing in 1964–5 by the Rose Society of Northern Ireland. Subsequently maintained by Belfast City Council Park Department, it evolved gradually and by the 1980s covered 4.5ha (11 acres) with 20,000 roses in regular beds. In

1987–9 the whole garden was redesigned to blend into the landscape and more recently more trellises were added, giving greater substance to the overall design.

The peak period for the garden is mid-July, when the final trials judging takes place. Trial winners occupy beds by the entrance approach into the garden, while nearby enormous floribunda displays spread out over the hill. Most of the trial beds are dotted around the park in concentric circles, enlivened with trellises and other timberwork. Near the house there is a special display tracing the history of the rose and elsewhere there are displays for climbing roses and heritage roses. The areas devoted to roses bred by McGredy's of Portadown and Dickson's of Newtownards may be considered to be of special interest. The McGredy nursery has produced a virtually unbroken series of floribundas, hybrid tea, and climbing roses since 1895, while the Dickson family have been rose breeders since 1879. Today Dickson's mostly produces floribundas, patio roses, and shrub roses rather than the classic hybrid roses of the past.

Other attractions of Wilmont include the international camellia trials, usually held in early April; the camellias are inside and outside the east of the walled garden. There is also a Japanese Garden and a selection of trees and shrubs in the grounds.

Rose displays enclosed by trellises and canopied supports in the heritage garden.

Key to gardens

1 Airfield
2 Ardcarraig
3 Ardgillan Demesne
4 Ballindoolin
5 Ballinlough
6 Beech Park
7 Belvedere
8 Birr Castle Demesne
9 Butterstream
10 Coolcarrigan
11 Dublin: Dillon Garden
12 Dublin: Iveagh Gardens

13 Dublin: National
      Botanic Gardens,
      Glasnevin
14 Dublin: St Anne's Park
15 Dublin: Trinity College
      Botanic Gardens
16 Dublin: War Memorial
      Gardens
17 Earlscliffe
18 Enniscoe House
19 Fairfield Lodge
20 Fernhill

21 Glebe Gardens:
      Ratoath
22 Hamwood
23 Knockree
24 Kylemore Abbey
25 Larchill
26 Lodge Park
27 Loughcrew
28 Marlay Park
29 Primrose Hill

30 Rockfield
31 Strokestown Park
32 Talbot Botanic Gardens:
      Malahide Castle
33 Tully: Japanese Gardens
34 Tullynally Castle

Key

═══ Motorways
─── Principal trunk highways
③ Gardens
⬤ Major towns and cities
• Towns

Central  *Ireland*

A map showing the gardens to be found in and near the city centre of Dublin.

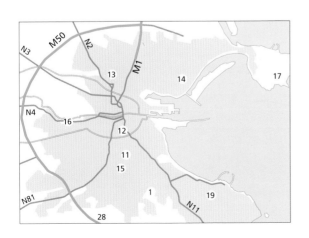

This region covers several distinct areas, including the midlands, the western counties, and the eastern seaboard, where the capital, Dublin, is situated. Historically, the area embraces the provinces of Connaught and North Leinster, divided centrally by the southward-flowing River Shannon.

Most of the gardens in this region are clustered around Dublin, the main population centre. Located in flat, fertile country drained by the River Liffey, Dublin has Ireland's driest weather (less than 75cm/30in of rain a year), with mean temperatures ranging from 5.5°C (42°F) in January to 16°C (61°F) in July. There are, however, surprising variations and some gardens can support a wide range of tender plants: at Earlscliffe (see p.64), the temperature never falls below -6°C (21°F), yet a few miles away at Glasnevin (see pp.58–61) it regularly falls to -10°C (14°F) and in 1982 it fell as low as -18.5°C (-1°F). However, these lows tend not to be sufficiently prolonged to kill less hardy plants.

41

The city and its environs boast over 100 public parks, the largest being St Anne's Park (see p.62) and Phoenix Park (710ha/1,752 acres). Many have their origins in Dublin's Georgian town planning, when St Stephen's Green and other elegant squares were laid out to provide "lungs for the city". In more recent years Dublin's County Council has resurrected this enlightened policy and acquired a ring of parks around the expanding city. These include a series of historic demesnes with good gardens, namely Ardgillan (see p.46), Talbot Botanic Gardens (see p.75), and Marlay Park (see p.72). Excellent programmes of restoration work have been undertaken at all three, while Dúchas – the Heritage Service – has brought back to life the War Memorial Gardens (see p.63), and Iveagh Gardens (see p.57), as well as undertaking a massive conservation programme at the National Botanic Gardens in Glasnevin (see pp.58–61). In addition, Dublin boasts many excellent private gardens open to the public, the most distinguished of these being the Dillon Garden (see p.56), Beech Park (see p.49), Primrose Hill (see p.72), and Fernhill (see pp.66–72).

To the west of Dublin lie the midlands, a great central plain studded with lakes, rivers, and bogs, which rarely rises above 100m (330ft). As this is a largely limestone and featureless area with winter temperatures regularly falling to -10°C (14°F), gardening can be a challenge. Yet the gardens here are of high quality, among them Birr (see pp.50-3), Strokestown Park (see p.74), and Ballinlough (see p.48). Similar adverse gardening conditions prevail in County Meath, Ireland's pastoral heartland, where there are also excellent gardens, most notably Butterstream (see pp.54–5.). Overcoming problems of wind and heavy rain in the western counties demands different solutions, which have been brilliantly overcome at Ardcarraig (see p.45), one of the best gardens in the whole country.

A teak Geisha House was imported from Japan in 1906 for Tully's Japanese Gardens.

 *Airfield*

open: 26 Apr to 30 Sep, Tue
to Sat, 12 noon–4pm

Further information from:
The Manager, Airfield, Dundrum,
Dublin 14
Tel: 01 2984301
Fax: 01 2962832
e-mail: airfield-trust@iol.ie

Nearby sights of interest:
Rathfarnham Castle: Easter
weekend Sat to Mon, 10am–5pm;
Apr, Sun, 10am–5pm; May to Oct,
daily, 10am–5pm; Tel: 01 4939462;
01 6613111 for winter opening
times; there are pleasant walks in
the mountains above Rathfarnham
(go via Stocking Lane) in Killakee
Demesne (Massey's Wood), and up
to the Hellfire Club.

Location: On E side of Dundrum towards Stillorgan, on S side of Upper Kilmacud Road; new entrance gates into car park

Airfield is an attractive 19th-century house set in 1.5ha (4 acres) of gardens with splendid views across old meadows to the Dublin Mountains. It may seem difficult to believe such a charming place could survive amid the suburban sprawl of Dundrum, but the property was left by the Overend sisters specifically to ensure that it remained to serve the public good. Letitia (born 1880) and Naomi (born 1900) were famous for their charity work, their herd of Jersey cattle, and their Rolls-Royce, which they maintained themselves and habitually parked in the middle of the village street.

Work on revitalizing the gardens began after the establishment of the Airfield Trust in 1993. The garden designer Arthur Shackleton was responsible for much of the early work, particularly to the walled garden below the house windows. Here an arbour was added, now festooned with old roses, such as the richly scented 'Lady Hillingdon' and the beautiful 'Comte de Chambord'. Around it is arranged a series of small, compartmented areas, including a pond, a herb garden, and colourful herbaceous borders. A border south of the wall contains *Abutilon vitifolium*, *Melaleuca armillaris*, and *Acca sellowiana* amid other tender plants, while to the east lies an orchard with old Irish cultivars, a melon house, and a Victorian conservatory filled with ferns and tender plants. Lawns in front of the house boast fine specimen trees, and a path of clipped yews shades a border which includes a good *Sophora microphylla*.

Spires of tall *Echium pininana* dominate the south border.

Ardcarraig

Location: Take second left off Galway–Moycullen road (after Kelehan's pub), and after 400m (¼ mile) house is ninth on left

Open: By appointment

Further information from:
Lorna McMahon, Ardcarraig,
Bushy Park, Oranswell,
Co Galway
Tel: 091 524336

Nearby sights of interest:
Aughnanure Castle, Oughterard:
mid-Jun to mid-Sep, daily,
9.30am–6.30pm; Tel: 091 82214;
Nora Barnacle Museum (Bowling
Green, off Shop Street, Galway):
mid-May to mid-Sep, Mon to Sat,
10am–5pm; Tel: 091 563746.

The design of this much-admired 1.5ha (4 acre) garden has transformed what was a rocky wasteland, providing an inexhaustible model for gardeners in bleak, wet, and windy environments. Its succession of compartments in hazel woodland is largely the creation of one woman, who began in 1971 with little more than a crowbar and determination.

The earliest and more conventional parts of the garden lie around the house, where maples, birch, and a beech hedge enclose a sloping lawn with specimen trees, notably a white-flowering *Crinodendron patagua*, and a succession of bulbs. A rocky hollow is devoted to dwarf conifers, interplanted with saxifrages, sea-pinks, and iberis, while above lies a large bed of heathers. Behind the house a small court boasts many climbers, such as the red-flowering *Berberidopis corallina* and the purple-leafed *Vitis* 'Brant', and leads into a knot garden for herbs. A sunken garden beyond has a large Cretan terracotta pot in the centre and a pergola on one side.

In true Robinsonian style the nature of the "wild garden" has been dictated by the landscape. Paths through hazel woodland proceed up to a rhododendron garden with roses, clematis, and perennial geraniums to follow. Steps flanked by azaleas head to a bog garden dominated by drifts of candelabra primulas, with lysichitons, meconopsis, irises, astilbes, and lobelias all enjoying the moist conditions. Little paths lead to a stream flanked with lily of the valley and water irises, and on to a wet area filled with hostas and ferns, including a collection of Australasian tree ferns. A Japanese-inspired "hill and pool" garden contains pools, exposed stones, and Japanese azaleas, maples, and cherries. A more recent garden, featuring plants donated by friends, was begun in 1997 to commemorate the owner's husband, Harry.

A snow lantern backed by acers reflected in the pond, with Mount Fuji (the triangular rock) behind.

Ardgillan Demesne

Location: Between Skerries and Balbriggan; signposted from main Belfast road

open: All year, daily; Nov to Jan, 10am–5pm; Feb to Mar, 10am–6pm; Apr, 10am–7pm; May, 10am–8pm; Jun to Aug, 10am–9pm; Sep, 10am–8pm; Oct, 10am–7pm. Guided tour of garden and conservatory, Jun to Aug, Thu, 3pm, or by appointment

open: All year, daily except Mon, 11am–6pm; open Bank Holiday Monday; closes 23 Dec to 1 Jan; admission charge.

Further information from:
The Administrator, Ardgillan Castle
Tel: 01 8492212
Fax: 01 8492786

Nearby sights of interest:
Newbridge Demesne; Tel: 01 436064; Newbridge House; Tel: 01 436534 or 01 727777 (Parks Dept).

The rose garden is overlooked by the conservatory and sheltered from the wind by hedges.

The battlemented 18th-century house of Ardgillan, one-time home of the Taylour family, is embosomed in 80ha (200 acres) of sweeping parkland offering fabulous panoramas of the sea. When the local council acquired the property in 1982 for a regional park, the gardens had long vanished, save for a fine walk of Florence Court yews of c1800. Today the gardens, covering about 2.5ha (6 acres), have been brought back almost to their former glory.

Strong easterly winds are a problem here, so a hedge of beech and *Cupressus* x *leylandii* 'Aurea' was planted between the castle and the rose garden. This is laid out in a geometrical arrangement of beds around a central water basin and contains disease-resistant hybrid tea and floribunda roses. There is a double line of rose pillars flanking the area with climbers, such as *Rosa rugosa* and *R. moyesii*, while old varieties, such as 'Empress Josephine', are planted around the walls. Also against the wall is a magnificent Scottish-made 1880s conservatory, which the council moved from nearby Seamount House in the 1990s.

The adjacent walled garden, which was derelict in 1982, is now back in full cultivation. It contains two free-standing walls, one of which has a series of 20 alcoves for the protection of fruit trees. Another wall has a pair of reconstructed greenhouses, while other areas contain alpines, flower borders, a geometrically laid-out *potager* with neat box edging, and a herb garden filled with old-fashioned herb varieties. Plant labelling is generally good throughout the garden.

 ## *Ballindoolin*

Location: 5km (3 miles) N of Edenderry on Kinnegad road (R401)

Ballindoolin is one of the "lost" gardens of Ireland which have blossomed into new life as a result of the Great Gardens of Ireland Restoration Programme. Visitors arrive by a long avenue that passes through attractive parkland and contains many old trees. The tall Georgian house, rear yards, and walled garden were all built together in 1821 by the Bor family of Dutch merchants, replacing an earlier house in the demesne.

As with most country houses of this period, the walled garden is approached through a pleasure ground dotted with ornamental trees. There is a cleared rock fernery, while access to the garden is through a newly built reception centre and restaurant. The walled garden, covering 0.8ha (2 acres), has been restored to its late 19th-century appearance and is typically dissected by formal, box-edged gravel paths, incorporating ornamental and working areas. A memorable feature is the magnificent apple espaliers, all apparently Dutch varieties and at least 150 years old, lining the paths and, as was the practice in 19th-century Irish kitchen gardens, shielding the vegetables from view. A beautifully restored feature of the period is the herbaceous border, running the 100m (330ft) length of the garden wall. Many of the other paths are lined with old-fashioned flower and shrub borders, including an impressive rose border at one end, while the area flanking the garden entrance has a large, circular, box-edged parterre with a central sundial. Outside the garden, fine parkland walks include a visit to a 1781 dovecote built in the shape of a shamrock.

open: May to Sep, daily except Mon, 12 noon–6pm; other times by appointment

open: Guided tours, May to Sep, daily except Mon, 12 noon–6pm

Further information from:
Ester Malony, Ballindoolin, Carbury, Co Kildare
Tel: 0405 31430
Fax: 0405 32377
e-mail: sundial@iol.ie
Website: www.ballindoolin.com
Restaurant: 0405 32400

Nearby sights of interest:
Ruins of Carbury Castle.

Ancient espaliered apple trees flank the walled garden's paths.

5 *Ballinlough*

Location: On N52 between Kells and Mullinga; signposted from Athboy

open: Tue to Thu, Sat and Bank Holidays, 11am–6pm, plus Sun, 1 May to 30 Sep, 2–6pm; closes first two weeks of Aug; other times by appointment

Further information from:
Sir John Nugent, Ballinlough Castle, Clonmellon, Co Westmeath
Tel: 046 33135
Tea Room: 046 33344
Fax: 046 33334
Head Gardener: Ursula Walsh
Fax: 046 33331

Nearby sights of interest:
Grove Gardens and Tropical Bird Sanctuary (between Kells and Athboy on R164, signposted): daily, 10am–6pm; Tel: 046 34276 (Pat and Therese Dillon); Taghmon Church; ruins of 15th-century church, Rathmore; Hill of Ward (ancient earthworks).

This beguiling castle, a mixture of 17th- and 18th-century reconstructions, has been in the same family since at least the 15th century. It overlooks a lake set in romantic 1780s parkland, whose features include woodland walks, a pleasure ground flanking a second lake, and a walled garden hidden behind the yards.

The walled garden, which has been the subject of an enormous restoration project since 1994, covers 1.2ha (3 acres) It is divided into four walled sections, with further subdivisions of beech hedging, so that the overall character is one of a series of linked compartments, each devoted to imaginative new planting designed by the well-known gardener Jim Reynolds. It includes a fruit garden with cordoned and espaliered fruit trees, a lily pond amid flowering cherries, and a magnificent double herbaceous border, forming a fine vista through the main garden. Magnolias have been planted nearby alongside a wisteria-draped south wall, while in the rose garden cruciform paths lined with *Lavandula stoechas* 'Papillon' and backed by old roses and lilies meet in a Gothic 'tent' festooned with the vigorous white rose *R. filipes* 'Kiftsgate'. A small adjacent garden is edged with mixed borders and its walls are draped with clematis and climbing hydrangeas.

Through a Gothick gate based on one at Prince Charles's garden at Highgrove, visitors can admire the many ornamental trees and shrubs of the pleasure ground adjoining the small lake. There are also a rock garden, a heather ground, and a wonderful rustic bridge, beyond which are lovely woodland walks.

The herbaceous border divides the main garden in the traditional manner.

Beech Park

Location: Near Luttrellstown at Clonsilla; entrance by railway station

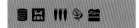

One of Ireland's greatest post-war plantsmen, the late David Shackleton, built up a vast collection of perennials in his 0.8ha (2 acre) walled garden. Apart from herbaceous material, it included numerous alpines in raised beds. After his death Jonathan and Daphne Shackleton successfully ran the garden until its sale in 1996. Cuttings and divisions of many plants were taken to Lakeview (see p.28), while the original collection survives in good order. Visitors now arrive by a back avenue and do not see the bleached-terracotta Regency house.

open: Sun and Mon, 2–6pm; other times by appointment

Further information from:
Catherine Burke, Head Gardener, Beech Park, Clonsilla, Co Dublin
Tel: 086 8522886 or 8220360

Nearby sights of interest:
Anna Liffey Mill (currently being restored); Phoenix Park; Primrose Hill Garden, Lucan.

Belvedere

Location: 6.5km (4 miles) S of Mullingar on Tullamore road

Probably the finest small-scale landscape park in Ireland, Belvedere occupies about 44ha (110 acres) of rolling glacial topography, with commanding views across Lough Ennell. Its focus is a modest Palladian house designed in the early 1740s by Richard Castle for Robert Rochfort, later the first Earl of Belvedere. The park's cleverly contrived layout survives very much intact, punctuated by romantic follies: the Jealous Wall, the Gothick Octagonal Gazebo, and the Gothick Arch, all of which epitomize the mid-18th-century taste for Elysian allusions. Thomas Wright of Durham (1711–86), the famous antiquarian and astronomer, came here in the 1740s, and at least one of the follies, the Gothick Arch, is his design. Recent conservation of the park has allowed new paths to be laid down for visitor access, and the follies have been subject to a programme of restoration,

The stable yard behind the Jealous Wall has recently been converted into an impressive reception centre, while the 19th-century walled garden to the east of the house has been completely revitalized. Old walls have been rebuilt, the paths relaid, a greenhouse added, and the borders filled with shrubs and perennials in an attempt to bring back a flavour of its Edwardian heyday.

open: All year; daily, Apr to Sep, 10.30am–7pm; Oct to Mar, 10.30–6pm
open: As above

Further information from:
The Manager, Belvedere, Westmeath County Council, Mullingar, Co Westmeath
Tel: 044 49060
Fax: 044 49002
Council office, Mullingar:
Tel: 044 40861
e-mail: info@belvedere-house.ie

The Gothick Arch, designed by Thomas Wright.

Birr Castle Demesne

Location: Birr

open: All year, daily, 9am–6pm

Not open to public

Further information from:
The Birr Scientific and Heritage
Foundation, Birr, Co Offaly
Tel: 050 920336
Fax: 050 921583
e-mail: info@birrcastle.com
Website: www.birrcastle.com

Nearby sights of interest:
Science Centre (in yard to
demesne); restored 1840s
telescope (in demesne); Birr
Heritage Centre in John's Hall
(John's Mall) May to Sep,
Tel: 050 920110; Birr is a
splendid Georgian planned
town, largely intact.

The gardens at Birr are harmoniously interwoven with a landscape park of 61ha (150 acres), whose lake, river, woodlands, open spaces, terraces, and walled garden incorporate a remarkable collection of rare trees and shrubs, many grown from seed. The focus of the layout is a delightful Gothicized castle, which backs onto the town and gazes dreamily over the parkscape across Vaubanesque fortifications. Terraces descend to the River Camcor below, while the great Gothic frame of the world's biggest 19th-century telescope dominates the open parkland.

Entry to the gardens is through an 1840s stable yard, cleverly adapted as a reception area incorporating

The "Leviathan" telescope, built in the park in 1841–4.

The terraces give a dramatic view over the River Camcor.

Steps lead to cloistered walks through pleached hornbeams in the formal garden.

A focal point for the formal garden is provided by Bavarian urns.

Birr Castle, seen from across the terraces.

The formal garden's Delphinium Border has a mix of herbaceous perennials with *D. elatum* hybrids grown at Birr.

The margins of the lake boast some fine plantings.

a Science Centre. The centre focuses on some of the many achievements of the Parsons family, notably those of William, the third Earl of Rosse, who built the great telescope between 1841 and 1844. It was his father, the second earl, who after the Union of 1800 remodelled the 17th-century castle that had been begun by his ancestor Sir Lawrence Parsons on the site of a medieval castle of the O'Carrolls. The old house was heightened, crenellated, and turned back to front so that it faced a newly created Brownian landscaped park, which was adorned with a lake amid trees, woodland screens, and a distant walled garden. To provide local employment during the Great Famine of the 1840s this lake was enlarged, while at the same time a massive military-style star-shaped fort was dug in front of the castle.

Although a fernery was added to the grounds in the 1850s, the gardens at Birr were not really developed until the fifth earl inherited the property in 1908. He had the moat between the castle and the river levelled to make garden terraces, and planted flowering trees and shrubs on the banks of the Camcor. Many of his plants derived from the 1914 sale of Veitch's of Chelsea, including a number of Wilson's Chinese introductions; some

survivors include a rare *Carrierea calycina* and a large *Magnolia delavayi* against the terrace walls. The fifth earl was killed in action in 1918, but his son Michael, the sixth earl, continued developing the gardens, becoming a renowned horticulturalist in his own right. With untiring determination he persued plants from the Himalayas and the Far East, subscribing to many plant expeditions and going to China himself. When he died in 1979 he left behind one of Ireland's best gardens, filled to the brim with introductions by Wilson, Forrest, Kingdon Ward, Henry, Rock and Yü Tse-tsun.

Birr's horticultural heartland lies along the river banks below the garden terraces and the 1810 suspension bridge, the earliest of its kind in Ireland. Among the area's fine magnolias are a number raised from seed collected at Nymans, in Sussex, England, home of Anne, Countess of Rosse, wife of the sixth earl. The magnificent columnar *Eucryphia* x *nymansensis* 'Nymansay' is here and the largest known example of a grey poplar (*Populus canescens*). A rare Chinese tree, *Ehretia dicksonii*, stands on the High Walk, with a Morinda spruce flanking the Lilac Walk beyond. The lakeside walk has a large *Cornus nuttallii* and one of the earliest Dawn redwoods in cultivation. Further north a restored Victorian fernery with jets of water may be viewed, and there is an excellent arboretum on the Tipperary side of the river.

The walled garden contains a pair of 9m (30ft) high box hedges, planted over 200 years ago and claimed by the *Guinness Book of World Records* to be the world's tallest. The south-east quarter contains a suite of recently restored formal gardens laid out in 1935 by Anne, Countess of Rosse. A boxwood parterre, enclosed by cloisters of pleached hornbeam *allées*, is central to this. *Magnolia* 'Michael Rosse' is here and nearby *Paeonia* 'Anne Rosse', a hybrid tree peony with yellow flowers streaked with red, one of the many important contributions that Birr Castle has made to horticulture in Ireland.

The herbaceous borders on the terraces of the castle were restored in 1999.

Butterstream

Location: Outskirts of Trim, off Kildalkey road

open: Apr to Sep, daily, 11am–6pm; groups by appointment at any time

Further information from:
Jim Reynolds, Trim, Co Meath
Tel: 046 36017
Fax: 046 31702

Nearby sights of interest:
Trim Visitor Centre (Mill Street): Jun to Sep, daily, 10am–6pm; Oct to May, Wed to Sun, 10am–6pm; all year for group bookings; Tel: 046 37227; Trim Castle (medieval); Trim Cathedral (keyholder: Thomas Sheridan, Effernagh).

Herbaceous borders overlooked by the Rapunzel Tower.

At Butterstream the visitor is drawn into a journey of discovery, as the garden gradually reveals itself through a series of interlinking compartments. Neatly clipped hedges and leafy screens, enclosures, linking paths, vistas, and follies all frame carefully manipulated masses of flower and leaf forms, giving maximum delight to the senses. Inspired by Sissinghurst, it has no grand setting or approach and has been reclaimed from the wildness: in this case fields from Jim Reynolds' family farm.

The earliest element of the garden is the rose garden, begun in 1970, whose box-edged path hides the legs of old-fashioned varieties, including many varieties of Bourbon, Alba and moss roses. Beneath grow lilies, crinums, nerines, and clematis to extend the garden's season. At one end an attractive lookout tower has been built overlooking a white garden, where agapanthus, delphiniums, astrantias, and campanulas are also bordered behind clipped box. A tiny Red and Yellow Garden contains the vibrant colours thought too difficult to mix in the herbaceous border, and nearby the woodland garden has numerous hostas (65 varieties), primulas, and a Gothick bridge over the stream. The centrepiece of the garden, the herbaceous borders, is laid out around an oval island bed and contain a magnificent succession of colour from

June to October. The thistle-like *Eryngium* x *zabelii* 'Donard Variety' may be found amid great clouds of mauve-blue *Campanula lactiflora*, while from here the eye is drawn to a croquet lawn with a summerhouse, festooned with *Rosa* 'François Juranville'. On one side is a classical pool garden, echoing designs by Harold Peto, while above a courtyard is flanked by matching classical pavilions facing down a pair of impressive canals and allées in the early 18th-century style.

 # *Coolcarrigan*

Location: 3km (2 miles) from Prosperous; signposted by Dagwell's pub

This is limestone country, more usually associated with horses than with gardening, so it may be a surprise to find such a splendid garden here. Extending over 4ha (10 acres) beside a handsome early-Victorian house, it contains over 2,500 shrubs and trees, mostly planted by the present owners since 1972, with help from the plantsman Sir Harold Hillier.

The tree-lined avenue to the house has a stupendous collection of bulbs, with peaty areas supporting late-flowering rhododendron hybrids. Terraced lawns by the house, flanked by a late-flowering herbaceous border, are dominated by glasshouses containing peaches, grapes, tomatoes, and pot plants. The arboretum and pleasure ground behind have a small pond, a yew temple, an axial vista with Doric columns at each end, and endless meandering paths, bordered by choice trees, shrubs, and bulbs. On the back avenue one may visit the family church, built in 1885 in an Irish Early Christian style.

open: Apr to Aug, by appointment for groups of four or more

open: Apr to Aug, Mon to Fri, by prior arrangement

Further information from:
Hilary Wilson Wright
Tel: 045 863512 or 01 8341141
Fax: 01 83441400

Nearby sights of interest:
Castletown House, Celbridge:
Tel: 01 6288252; Maynooth
Ecclesiastical Museum: by
appointment; Tel: 045 431109.

A side lawn flanked by herbaceous borders and a Victorian glasshouse.

Dublin: Dillon Garden

Location: Turn right off Sandford Road at Merton Road Church; entrance in cul-de-sac

open: Mar, Jul and Aug, daily, 2–6pm; Apr to Jun and Sep, Sun, 2–6pm

Further information from:
The Hon Helen Dillon,
45 Sandford Road, Dublin 6
Tel: 01 4971308
Fax: 01 4971308

Nearby sights of interest:
Rathfarnham Castle: Easter weekend Sat to Mon, 10am–5pm; Apr, Sun, 10am–5pm; May to Oct, daily, 10am–5pm; Tel: 01 4939462; 01 6613111 for winter opening.

Surrounding a suave 1830s town house, this enchanting garden of 0.3ha (¼ acre) is the most admired and influential in Ireland. Its creator, Helen Dillon, an accomplished plantswoman and passionate gardener, is a household name through her books, television appearances, and above all her garden, which has received floods of praise from visiting gardeners from all parts of the world.

The garden was begun in the early 1970s when Helen and her husband Val moved here. Over the years it has continually evolved, though it has always been noted for superlative standards of gardening and a strong sense of colour and design. Herbaceous plants predominate, but alpines and bulbs play a key role in the succession of colour and scent from March to September. Plants are frequently moved to create better effects, and Herculean efforts are made to obtain unusual specimens, including regular plant expeditions to remote parts of the world. However, the rare and the common are freely interwoven and no plant is allowed to remain unless it positively contributes to this impeccable garden.

Spring is dominated by spectacular displays of hellebores, primulas, anemones, erythroniums, tulips, trilliums, and all members of the poppy family. Midsummer is the high point, however, when borders flanking the central lawn glisten with shades of soothing blue on one side and sizzling reds opposite. Catmints, delphiniums, and galegas play a major role in the blue border, helped by campanulas, cornflowers, salvias, eryngiums, and asters. Among the reds are penstemons, crocosmias, dahlias, and heucheras, mixed with cannas, tiger lilies, and roses, notably the tall, arching *R. glauca*. At the end of the lawn a circular fountain is backed by a bower of mixed roses, off which is a clematis pergola, a sundial garden with celmisias and agapanthus, and a yellow garden with gold-streaked hostas, euryops and day lilies. Close to the house is a glasshouse and nearby are numerous terracotta containers for alpines and succulents.

View of the path that lies behind the Red Border.

 # *Dublin: Iveagh Gardens*

Location: Access from Earlsfort Terrace and Clonmel Street (off Harcourt Street)

Designed as a splendid 6ha (15 acre) setting for Dublin's enormous International Exhibition of Arts and Manufacture in 1865, this garden quietly slumbered for over a century. In the 1990s it was the subject of a major restoration programme to revive Ninian Niven's grand formal scheme, which had consciously included the period's latest horticultural skills and styles.

The central portion of the garden is dominated by an axial path leading from the statue-studded terrace, which once fronted the exhibition building. On each side are circular basins and statuary fountains in the centre of sunken panels that once contained floral parterres. The vista terminates in a massive waterfall, with a rock-work design incorporating river gods in cavities, based on Hubert Robert's Bains d'Apollon at Versailles. Northerly paths from here lead to the sunken archery green overlooked by a gazebo, while southerly paths lead to a wooded area containing a series of restored gardens: a small labyrinth, a colourful rosarium, and the American Ground with many North American species. Scattered through this area are huge piles of stones, while the garden's perimeter is enclosed by earth banks to hide the streets outside.

open: Summer, Mon to Sat, 8.15am–6pm; Sun and Bank Holidays, 10am–6pm; winter, as above but closes half an hour before dusk

Further information from:
Margaret Gormley, Dúchas – The Heritage Service, St Stephen's Green, Dublin 2
Tel: 01 4757816

Nearby sights of interest:
National Museum and Natural History Museum, Merrion Street, Dublin 2, May to Sep, Tue to Sun, 10am–5pm; Oct, Sun, 1–5pm; Tel: 01 2800969; 29 Lower Fitzwilliam Street (restored Georgian house): all year except two weeks before Christmas, Tue to Sat, 10am–5pm, Sun 2–5pm; Tel: 01 7026165.

The Goddesses of Arts and Industry hold torches aloft for *jets d'eau*.

Dublin: National Botanic Gardens, Glasnevin

13

Location: Between Finglas Road and Botanic Road

open: All year, Mon to Sat,
9am–6pm, Sun, 11am–6pm
(4.30pm in winter); closes 25 Dec

Further information from:
National Botanic Gardens, Dúchas
– The Heritage Service, Glasnevin,
Dublin 9
Tel: 083 74388
Fax: 083 60080

Nearby sights of interest:
Casino at Marino (Malahide Road):
Feb to mid-Jun and Nov, Wed and
Sun, 12 noon–4pm; mid-Jun to
Sep, daily, 9.30am–6.30pm; Oct,
daily, 10am–5pm; Tel: 01 8331618;
Phoenix Park Visitor Centre: Jan
to mid-Mar, Sat and Sun,
9.30am–4.30pm; mid to end Mar,
daily, 9.30am–5pm; Apr to May,
daily, 9.30am–5.30pm; Jun to Sep,
daily, 9.30am–6.30pm; Oct, daily,
9.30am–5pm; Nov and Dec, daily,
9.30am–4.30pm; Tel: 01 6770095.

The National Botanical Gardens at Glasnevin, Ireland's premier botanical and horticultural establishment, occupies an attractive site of 19ha (48 acres) on the banks of the River Tolka. Founded by the (Royal) Dublin Society with the support of Parliament in 1795, it was designed to "promote a scientific knowledge of the various branches of agriculture". Subsequently its main purpose has been to maintain plant collections for both scientific and educational purposes, and it currently possesses more than 20,000 different plant species and cultivars.

The original botanic gardens were laid out by their first director,

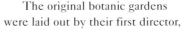

The Chain Tent, added in 1834–5, is draped with wisteria.

The Rock Garden, home to a fine collection of alpines.

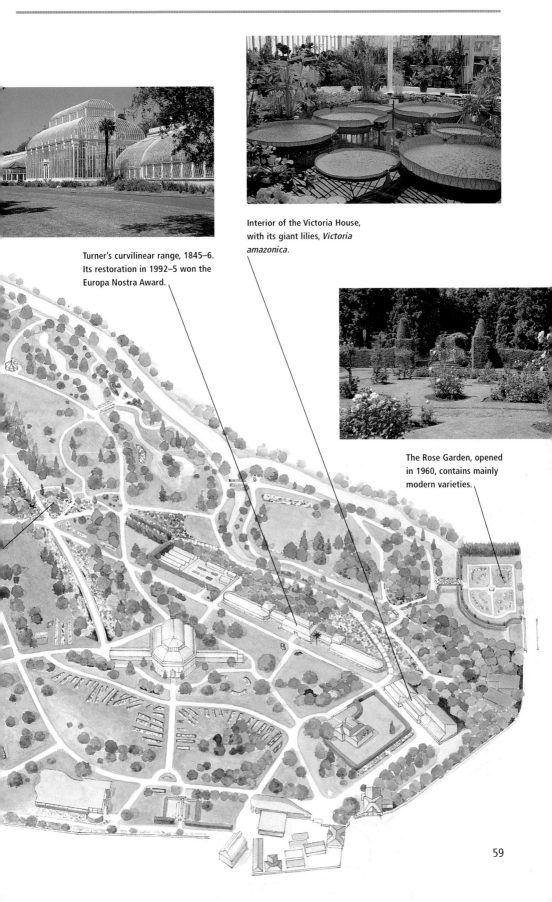

Interior of the Victoria House, with its giant lilies, *Victoria amazonica*.

Turner's curvilinear range, 1845–6. Its restoration in 1992–5 won the Europa Nostra Award.

The Rose Garden, opened in 1960, contains mainly modern varieties.

Addison's Yew Walk, planted around 1720, predates the Botanic Gardens.

The long twin herbaceous borders are colourful, although limited in content.

Walter Wade, but after his death they declined, to be resurrected and redesigned by Ninian Niven in 1834–8. Further modifications were carried out by later directors, Dr David Moore (1838–79), Sir Frederick Moore (1879–1922), J W Besant (1922–44), Dr T J Walsh (1944–68), and A Brady (1968–96). The gardens came into state care in 1878 and since 1992 have been run by the Office of Public Works, now part of Dúchas – The Heritage Service.

As the soil is alkaline, calcifuge plants are confined to peat beds, but the gardens enjoy a wide range of habitats, which are incorporated within a botanical rather than geographical layout. Special areas are devoted to ground-cover plants, economic and poisonous plants, native plants, herbs, and common and exotic vegetables. Among many of the collections are bearded irises, deutzias, peonies, chaenomeles and clematis, the latter on a trellis enclosing magnolias. The genus *Rosaceae* is prominent, including pyrus, malus and sorbus, and apart from large tree collections there are a rockery, principally for alpines, a Burren garden, a bog garden, and a pond for aquatic plants.

The finest of the glasshouses is the curvilinear range, built in 1845–6, and extended in 1868–9, by the ironmaster Richard Turner. Rebuilt in 1992–5, it houses a range of tender subjects, including cycads, podocarps, and a wonderful Cashmir cypress. The Great Palm House was built in 1884 and one of its side wings houses an outstanding orchid collection. Amazon water

lilies are housed in the Victorian House, built for them in 1854, flanked by a Cactus and Succulent House and a Fern House, containing the rare Killarney fern *Trichomanes speciosum*. A modern Alpine House lies near the new reception centre, while in the shade of a magnificent Persian elm, *Zelkova carpinifolia*, stands the National Herbarium Building, which contains 600,000 specimens and a horticultural library. A big attraction is the *Rosa chinensis* 'Old Blush' that inspired Thomas Moore's famous ballad.

The pond was dug in 1809–10 to accommodate aquatic plants.

Dublin: St Anne's Park

Location: Access in Mount Prospect Avenue, off Clontarf Road

open: All year

Further information from:
Ms D Hayden, Dublin Corporation, Dublin
Tel: 01 6723438 or 086 8150538

Nearby sights of interest:
Casino at Marino (off Malahide Road): Feb to mid-Jun and Nov, Wed and Sun, 12 noon–4pm; mid-Jun to Sep, daily, 9.30am–6.30pm; Oct, daily, 10am–5pm; Tel: 01 8331618.

Brilliant displays of climbing roses are found outside the main rose amphitheatre.

St Anne's Park, best known for its rose garden, was formerly the setting for Ireland's most palatial Victorian house. It is now a public park, but the 1880s house, built by Lord Ardilaun, was demolished in 1968. A radius of avenues, once aligned on the house, dissects the park amid extensive plantations of evergreen oaks. The walled garden, close to the house site, has a replica of a dwelling from Herculaneum and yew hedges. Among the many features below the house site are an artificial lake with Pompeian-style temple, a Gothick bridge, and a hermitage beside a cascaded stream.

St Anne's is commemorated with a bushy, white, single-flowering rose, 'Souvenir de St Anne's', found in Lady Ardilaun's garden. This rose, introduced by Graham Thomas in 1950, inspired Dublin Corporation to develop part of the grounds for international rose seedlings trials in the 1970s. An extensive rose garden was created around a vast sunken amphitheatre, incorporating massed displays of hybrid teas and floribundas with pergolas at the entrances. The rose trials in mid-July complement those in Belfast where the entries are drawn from catalogued varieties.

15 *Dublin: Trinity College Botanic Gardens*

Location: 4km (2½ miles) S of city centre, on SW side of Palmerston Park

 **open:** Mon to Fri, 9am–5pm; preferably by appointment

Further information from:
School of Botany, Trinity Botanical Gardens, Dartry, Dublin
Tel: 01 972070

Nearby sights of interest:
Mount Jerome Cemetery; Irish Jewish Museum, 3–4 Walworth Road, Portobello: May to Sept, Sun, Tue, and Thu, 11am–3.30pm; Oct to Apr, 10.30am–2.30pm; Tel: 01 4531797 or 4758388.

Although these botanical gardens were founded in the 17th century, they have occupied their present home in the attractive grounds of Trinity Hall only since 1967. There are lawns, attractive borders, and many interesting trees, some moved from their old home, including a striking *Meliosma dilleneifolia*. Glasshouse ranges contain collections of ferns; plants of Irish origin, including the cottonweed *Otanthus maritimus*; saxifrages; European wild plants; and desert and semi-desert plants, such as elephant's foot. In the tropical houses there is a fine collection of plants from Mauritius collected by the college in 1985.

16 *Dublin: War-Memorial Gardens*

Location: Just S of Islandbridge; access also through St John of God Church

 **open:** All year, daily, during daylight hours

Further information from:
Tony Connolly, Park Ranger, War Memorial Gardens, Islandbridge
Tel: 01 6770236

Nearby sights of interest:
Phoenix Park; Kilmainham Royal Hospital; Kilmainham Gaol.

This magnificent architectural ensemble occupies an 8ha (20 acre) site on the south slope of the River Liffey. Built between 1933 and 1939 to a monumental classical design in granite by Sir Edwin Lutyens, it later fell into decline and by the 1970s had become a forgotten wilderness. Restoration from the mid-1980s has transformed the site into one of Ireland's great showpieces.

The garden's main enclosure, whose long axis lies parallel to the river, contains the Stone of Remembrance, flanked by great circular fountain basins with obelisks. Imposing flights of steps lead up to the Cross of Sacrifice on one side, while at each end lies a pair of pavilions, one pavilion for each of the four provinces, bearing the names of 49,400 Irish soldiers lost in World War I. The pavilions, linked by colonnaded pergolas, overlook identical sunken gardens with central lily ponds and enclosing yew hedges. These are filled with hybrid tea roses, including Meilland's famous 'Peace' rose, produced in 1945. Lines of *Prunus* 'Ukon', 'Hisakura', and 'Watereri' stretch out into a 60ha (150 acre) park along the river banks, criss-crossed by avenues of golden poplars, silver limes, and Norway and silver maples.

Colonnades draped in wisteria and clematis, with an underplanting of lavender and santolina.

63

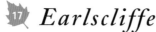

Earlscliffe

Location: Baron's Brae, Ceanchor Road, on S side of Howth Peninsula

open: Groups, by appointment only

Further information from:
Dr David Robinson, Baron's Brae, Ceanchor Road, Earlscliffe, Baily, Co Dublin
Tel: 01 8322556
Fax: 01 8323021
e-mail: davidrobinson@eircom.net
Website: www.earlscliffe.com

Nearby sights of interest:
Malahide Castle and gardens; Lusk Heritage Centre: mid-Jun to mid-Sep, 10am–6pm; Tel: 01 8437683.

Benefiting from a microclimate that is exceptionally mild for this latitude (53° 3″ N) and almost as favourable as Tresco in Cornwall, Earlscliffe boasts a range of plants that is unique in Ireland. The garden was started in 1969 within the grounds of an 1840s house and covers over 3ha (7.5 acres), extending above the cliffs and offering panoramic views south across Dublin Bay.

The garden is planned as a series of linked rooms with planting that reflects the scientific interests of Dr David Robinson, who enjoys growing plants to their climatic limits. He has demonstrated that many tender subjects can survive in his garden, such the umbrella tree *Schefflera digitata*, tree ferns such as *Cyathea dealbata* and *Dicksonia antarctica*, the Bunya bunya (*Araucaria bidwillii*) from Queensland, and *Strobilanthes pentastemonoides* from India. The red-blossomed *Echium wildpretii* grows here, and there are forests of *Echium pininana*, which self-seeds everywhere. Many species of puya, metrosideros, banksia, and at least 50 eucalyptus all thrive, including the beautiful *E. ficifolia*. Some may disagree with Dr Robinson's strong advocacy of simazine to kill weeds, but his remarkable success in growing so many tender plants speaks for itself.

Part of the upper garden area, looking out to sea.

Enniscoe House

Location: 3km (2 miles) S of Crossmolina on Pontoon and Castlebar road

open: Apr to Sep

Standing beneath the brooding mass of Mount Nephin, Enniscoe is an appealing 18th-century mansion set in a romantic landscape park covering 80ha (200 acres), whose woods and meadows sweep down to Lough Conn. Five generations of Jacksons lived here until 1834, when the property passed to the Pratt family, who were keen and knowledgeable gardeners. They created a 1.5ha (4 acre) pleasure ground south of the house in the 1870s and later remodelled the walled garden into a 0.8ha (2 acre) kitchen garden and a 0.5ha (1 acre) ornamental garden. In 1996–9 the present owner, a descendant of the Pratts, embarked on the restoration of these gardens, abandoned since 1950. Beneath dense growth most of the garden's features were found to be still intact. Extensive areas of rockery alpine beds were subsequently replanted, and nearby the large glasshouse range bases have been used as platforms for potted plants. Opposite, a rustic stone archway, a focal feature of the garden, was replanted with hardy ferns, while the garden's perimeter beds have been re-established with Edwardian-style mixed borders. The lawns, box-lined pathways, and summer bedding were also all accurately recreated using both field and photographic evidence.

Further information from:
Susan Kellett, Enniscoe House,
Castlehill, Ballina, Co Mayo
Tel: 096 31112
Fax: 096 31773
e-mail: enniscoe@indigo.ie

Nearby sights of interest:
Genealogy centre (in yard of Enniscoe House); Céide Fields Heritage Centre, Ballycastle;
Tel: 096 43325

The walled garden has been restored to its Edwardian form.

Fairfield Lodge

Location: Near top of Monkstown Avenue, on left

open: May to Sep, Wed, Sun and Bank Holidays, 2–6pm; other times by appointment

The maxim that small gardens need strong design is beautifully illustrated by this enchanting town garden attached to a small Georgian house. The tiny front garden successfully balances structure with seasonal colour, while a small side garden cleverly uses a combination of cool greens and yellow to give the illusion of space and light. Prominent plants include golden hollies, spireas, hops, and Spanish gorse. The back lawn is surrounded by tall shrubs and garden trees, such as a mimosa *Acacia dealbata*, crinodendrons, and leptospermums, while herbaceous plants are used for colour in front. An elegant urn closes the vista.

Further information from:
John Bourke, Monkstown Avenue,
Dublin
Tel: 01 2803912 or 087 2707719 (mobile)
Fax: 01 2803912
e-mail: jsb@indigo.ie
Website: www.dublingardens.com

 **20** *Fernhill*

open: Mar to Sep, Tue to Sat
and Bank Holidays, 11am–5pm,
Sun, 2–6pm

Further information from:
Mrs Sally Walker, Fernhill,
Sandyford, Co Dublin
Tel: 01 2956000 or 087 2436494
(mobile)

Nearby sights of interest:
Ballyedmunduff megalithic tomb
(National Monument);
Powerscourt house, gardens, and
waterfall (see pp.104–7).

The rock garden, situated
above the house, is filled
with herbaceous perennials,
dwarf shrubs, and bulbs.

Location: On main Enniskerry road (R117) between Lambs Cross and Stepaside

Fernhill is particularly noted for its outstanding collection of camellias, magnolias, and rhododendrons, but this 16ha (40 acre) garden has much more to offer, not least its superb panoramas across Dublin Bay. Its wooded, sloping grounds contain a wide collection of flowering trees and shrubs, together with a rockery, heather garden, fernery, water garden, and kitchen garden, as well as wonderful drifting clouds of spring bulbs.

The demesne has 18th-century origins, but the garden's bones were created in the second half of the 19th century by the Darley family. They laid out the straight Broadwalk, flanked by many fine trees, including an enormous *Tsuga heterophylla* and a good *Dacrydium cupressinum*. Beneath the trees are many old rhododendrons, such as an excellent bright-blue *R. augustinii* and the original pink-flowering 'Fernhill Silver'. There are superb examples of *R. genestierianum*, tender, white-flowering *R. lindleyi*, and a well-developed *Michelia doltsopa* from China. In this area is the laurel lawn, a rarely seen survivor from the Victorian era and still beautifully clipped. Other attractions from that era include a kitchen garden with a *potager*-style layout.

The garden's modern pre-eminence is due to Susan and the late Ralph Walker. From 1934 they added many new areas, increasing the collections and adopting a Robinsonian style of planting. Many more rhododendrons were planted with varieties of camellia, pieris, and leptospermum. A heather bank was made on the slopes above the house, where *Bergenia* 'Ballawley' grows: a surviving cultivar from the long-vanished nursery at nearby Ballawley. The old adjacent rockery was transformed and planted with pieris, cordylines, bulbs, perennials, azaleas, and a variety of alpines, and a narrow stream was diverted to make ponds. The planting above includes ferns, pulmonarias, and some of Mrs Walker's famed collection of primulas.

21 *Glebe Gardens: Ratoath*

Location: Lane access opposite gate to Catholic church in Ratoath

Behind the ruins of the Protestant church in Ratoath there are two separate and distinct gardens, whose owners find it convenient to market their gardens as one unit.

The earlier house, Glebelands, is a handsome, gable-ended block of c1813, clad with roses and approached by a tree-lined avenue. It is set in undulating land, emphasized by low stone walling and mature trees augmented with 1970s plantings of blue cedars, pines, conifers, acers, and larches. A pergola to one side leads past a colourful display of shrub roses to the back garden. This is a small, enclosed lawn overlooking a terrace and surrounded by mixed borders; it is rather dark in the afternoon.

Much of the mature planting at Glebelands was undertaken by a local architect, Arthur Lardner, who lived here until 1990, when he moved into a modern house he built for himself a few fields away. This garden, Glebewood, covers 0.5ha (1¼ acres) of flat, featureless land, but has been radically transformed with earth banks and landscaping to create a series of interlinking but discrete areas. From the house a pergola festooned with roses leads to a sparkling display of shrub and standard roses enclosing a statue of Diana. Beyond, the garden's perfect green lawns flow around swirls of beds, filled with stunning and immaculately maintained displays of shrubs and perennials.

open: Easter Sun to end Sep, Wed to Sun, 2–6pm; guided tours 2pm and 4.30pm; other times by appointment

Further information from:
Arthur Lardner and Carmel Heslin, Ratoath, Co Meath
Tel: 01 8256015 or 8256219

Nearby sights of interest:
Hill of Tara; Tel: 046 25903.

Lavender surrounds Diana in Glebewood's rose garden.

open: Apr to Aug, Mon to Fri, and third Sun of each month, 2–6pm

Further information from:
Major Hamilton
Tel: 01 8255210

Nearby sights of interest:
Maynooth Castle (keyholder: Mrs Saults, 9 Parson Street); Maynooth Ecclesiastical Museum: by appointment; Tel: 045 431109.

Hamwood

Location: 3km (2 miles) from Dunboyne on Maynooth road, by Ballymacoll Stud

This is a small Palladian house built in 1768 by the Hamiltons, who were agents to the Dukes of Leinster. Its front lawn leads to a straight walk lined with conifers, including good specimens of *Cedrus deodara*, *Betula alba laciniata*, *Cupressus macrocarpa* (planted 1844), and *Pinus monticola* (planted 1847). Below are camellias, magnolias, shrub roses, euphorbias, acers, and spring bulbs. The back lawn has rose beds in a geometric layout of c1860, while the walled garden contains a rock garden of c1820, a somewhat wild Edwardian rose garden, and a number of notable trees and shrubs, including a *Cornus florida*, a golden Philadelphus, and a good davidia.

open: 1 Apr to 16 Jul, by appointment

Further information from:
Mrs Shirley Beatty
Tel: 01 2955884
Fax: 01 2955884
e-mail: jsb@indigo.ie
Website: www.dublingardens.com

The planting can be admired from various secluded viewpoints.

Knockree

Location: Carrickmines; SW of Foxrock and Cabinteely, one third of way up Glenamuck Road, between Enniskerry and Brighton/Brennanstown roads

Much of the character of this 0.8ha (2 acre) garden is determined by its site, on gently sloping ground covered with huge glacial boulders. Such topography might seem an insurmountable obstacle to creating a garden, but at Knockree the boulders have been skilfully used to create backdrops and focal points amid a tapestry of colourful planting.

The garden was started by the present owner in the early 1960s and is divided into distinct areas. Below the house there are lawns with borders where hellebores and meconopsis do well amid shrubs and climbing roses. An enormous granite rock dominates the upper area, where rhododendrons, acers, and colourful perennials emerge from the rocky hollows. The garden is best in spring, but there is interest all year, with many rare and unusual plants and excellent collections of hardy geraniums, roses, primulas, ferns, and grasses. At the top of the garden the planting gives way to wild boulders and a mountain panorama.

Kylemore Abbey

Location: From N59, just past Recess, turn right on to R344; signposted

The sense of an enchanted fairy tale prevails at this imposing baronial castle, whose numerous battlements and turrets rise romantically above the waters of a lake, amid the splendour of the barren Connemara mountains. It was built in the late 1860s by Mitchell Henry, a Manchester financier and MP, whose vast expenditure included building a model farm, planting millions of trees, and constructing a magnificent 2.5ha (6 acres) walled garden. This was located about 1.5km (1 mile) west of the castle in a dramatic but sheltered position and contained ornamental grounds, kitchen stuff, and a series of spectacular glasshouses forming three sides of a terrace.

In the 20th century the garden was gradually abandoned, and was a jungle by 1996 when the Benedictine nuns who have owned Kylemore since 1920 began an ambitious restoration programme. After clearance and archaeological excavations, the old garden's features were exposed, including the bases of the great wooded glasshouses. A number of the glasshouses have now been restored, together with a castellated bothy and the gardener's house, while the elaborate island bedding scheme in the lawns has regained its 1870s appearance. In the west half of the garden, screened by beeches, chestnuts, and sycamores along a stream, the old layout of vegetable plots separated by paths has been re-established, along with a fine herbaceous border running through the centre.

open: Mid-Mar to Oct, 10am–5.30pm
open: All year, 9am–5.30pm

Further information from:
Bridgette Brew, Kylemore Abbey,
Connemara, Co Galway
Tel: 095 41146
Fax: 095 411145
e-mail: enquiries @kylemoreabbey.ie
Website: www.kylemireabbey.com

Nearby sights of interest:
Letterfrack and Connemara
National Park: Easter, Apr, May
and Sep, daily, 10am–5.30pm;
Jun, 10am–6.30pm; Jul and Aug,
9.30am–6.30pm; last admission
45 minutes before closing;
Tel: 095 41006; Dan O'Hara
Heritage Centre, Lettershea,
Clifden: Apr to Sep, daily,
10am–6pm; Tel: 095 21246
or 21808.

The restored floral arch and its formal bedding.

Larchill

open: May to Sep, daily, 12 noon to 6pm

Further information from:
Michael and Louisa de las Casas, Kilcock, Co Kildare
Tel: 01 6287354
Fax: 01 6284580
e-mail: delascas@indigo.ie

Nearby sights of interest:
Maynooth Castle and College; Taghadoe Round Tower.

The miniature sham fort, known as Gibraltar, in the lake.

Location: 32km (20 miles) W of Dublin, on N4; turn right to Kilcock on Dunshaughlin road

When restoration of this mid-18th-century park began in 1994, its remarkable follies and garden buildings were thickly embedded in undergrowth, while its lake was little more than a boggy field. By 1998 an award-winning reconstruction programme had miraculously reinstated this exhilarating piece of lost Arcadia.

The park's history is shrouded in mystery, but on stylistic grounds it is clearly an early example of the "natural" landscape style, c1740–50. A circular walk enclosing the 25ha (63 acre) park begins in a Gothic ornamental farmyard and passes a series of crude but attractive follies, including the tall "shell tower", the temple-like Fox's Earth, a tree-clad mound, a sham ruined boathouse, a temple-like gazebo, and a Biddulph-style Chinese bridge. There are castellated sham fort and a temple in the lake, plus a statue of Bacchus. By the house a substantial walled garden, noted for its open loggia "dairy", has been colourfully replanted, while the park has become home to the largest collection of rare breeds of farm animals in Ireland.

 Lodge Park

open: Jun and Jul, Tue to Fri and Sun, 2–6pm; Aug, Tue to Fri, 2.30–5.30pm; other times by appointment

Further information from:
Mrs Sarah Guinness, Lodge Park, Straffan, Co Kildare
Tel: 01 6288412 or 6273155
Fax: 01 6273477
e-mail: garden@steam-museum.ie
Website: www.steam-museum.ie

Nearby sights of interest:
The Steam Museum (adjacent to walled garden).

Location: From Maynooth and Lucan, take N4 to Straffan, then follow signs to Steam Museum, 1.5km (1 mile) from village

Handsome parkland surrounds the Palladian house at Lodge Park, but the object of chief interest is the 1ha (2½ acre) walled garden, which is discreetly located close to the house and, like it, probably dates to around 1773. For nearly two centuries it had provided fruit, vegetables, and cut flowers for the house, and like so many other Irish walled gardens was also adapted as a pleasure ground. However, it had become neglected by 1982, when the present owners embarked on a major restoration. The old path layout was retained, and while the garden has been developed in an individual way the traditional ethos of combining "beauty and utility" within its walls has been retained.

The internal design of the garden is dictated by a main axial path running alongside the south-facing wall borders. Regularly spaced clipped yews and low box hedging line the path, with shrub borders and asparagus beds on one side and a series of garden compartments opposite. Immediately inside the garden gate, framed with white wisteria, lies the "white garden", centred on an old carved-stone well-head with white forms of buddleia, Japanese anemones, agapanthus, foxgloves, 'Iceberg' roses, and *Campanula persicifolia*. Opposite stands a restored classical orangery containing tender clematis, daturas, plumbagos, and *Acnistus australis*, and nearby is a geometric "salad garden" centred on a former stone sundial. The latter is flanked by a sweet-pea pergola and an espaliered walk, with areas for vegetables and fruit beyond. In an orchard at the end of this walk a metal, tent-like rosarium is festooned with old climbing roses, including the white 'Rambling Rector'. Beyond a beech hedge lies a south-facing herbaceous border.

Mixed herbaceous border with penstemons, phloxes, onopordums, agastaches, and a big *Crambe cordifolia*.

27 *Loughcrew*

Location: Off N3, 5km (3 miles) from Oldcastle off Mullingar road

At Loughcrew the remains of a Norman motte, a medieval church, and residual features of a late 17th-century manor give character to a recently restored Victorian pleasure ground. About 800m (½ mile) distant lie the ruins of the 1823 Loughcrew house, built by the architect C R Cockerell for J L Naper and destroyed by fire in 1960. Its portico was re-erected in 1998 as an eye-catcher in the park, all dramatically overlooked by the Loughcrew Hills and their famous prehistoric passage-grave cemeteries.

The 2.5ha (6 acre) pleasure ground was laid out in the area south of the walled garden, with lawns, specimen trees, a pond, and a stream planted with primulas. A focal point is the walled garden gate and surround, which may have come from the Napers' late 17th-century house close by. Brilliantly colourful herbaceous borders have been replanted along the length of the wall, flanked by a narrow canal and urns. At one end lie a thatched summerhouse and a "grotesque" rock fernery while, nearby, water emerges from under a cedar by a pond. An avenue of yews to the south was probably planted as part of a formal garden layout in the early 18th century. The garden contains modern sculpture and has been imaginatively used to stage operas.

open: Apr, May and Sep to mid-Oct, Fri to Sun and Bank Holidays, 11am–6pm; Jun to Aug, daily, 11am–6pm; groups by appointment

Further information from:
Charles and Emily Naper, Loughcrew, Oldcastle, Co Meath
Tel: 049 8541922
Fax: 049 8541722
e-mail: cnaper@tinet.ie

Nearby sights of interest:
Loughcrew Megalithic Cemetery (keyholder: Basil Balfe, St Oliver's, Newtown, Oldcastle).

28 *Marlay Park*

Location: S of Rathfarnham and E of Ballyboden on Grange road, past Grange Golf Club; entrance off very busy road

open: April–September; telephone for opening times

open: As above

Further information from: Dun Laoghaire-Rathdowne County Council, Co Dublin
Tel: 01 4934059 or 2054700
e-mail: dshannon@dlrcoco.ie

Nearby sights of interest: Rathfarnham Castle; Tel: 01 4939462.

The restored walled gardens at Marlay were built in the 1790s at the same time as the house was remodelled and set in a landscape park with lakes and a *cottage orné*. The estate belonged to the La Touche family, successful French Huguenot bankers until 1864, and subsequently passed through a number of hands before being acquired by the local county council as a regional park in 1972. Two sections of the walled garden have been closely restored to a Regency appearance with an orangery, fountains, and flowerbeds filled with plants known from the period. The old gardener's house has been cleverly adapted as the entrance to the garden.

29 *Primrose Hill*

Location: W of Lucan off main road; entrance after bridge and traffic lights

open: Feb and mid-Jun to mid-Aug, daily, 2–6pm; groups by appointment

Further information from: Mrs Hall, Primrose Hill, Lucan, Co Dublin
Tel: 01 6280373

Nearby sights of interest: Phoenix Park Visitor Centre.

Herbaceous borders brimming with colour and interest.

This garden was started by Cicely Hall around her Regency house in Lucan in the early 1950s and has subsequently become one of the best plantsman's gardens in Ireland. In spring and summer it is a carpet of brilliant hues of countless perennials, all happily intermixed and overflowing the paths. Pride of place goes to Irish plants, such as the glorious *Meconopsis* x *sheldonii* 'Slieve Donard' and rarities such as *Astrantia* 'Old Irish Blue'. There is a selection of *Kniphofia* variants, including *K. snowdenii*, Nankeen lilies, herbaceous lobelias, and some lovely old roses.

Undoubtedly Primrose Hill is best known for its snowdrops (*Galanthus*), which are one of the principal passions of Cicely's son Robin. These are found both in the rear gardens and across the front lawns beneath the beech trees. They include the 'Primrose Hill Specials' and the famous 'Straffan'. Others to note include the double Irish cultivar 'Hill Poë', 'Merlin', *G. nivalis* Poculiformis Group, and *G. reginae-olgae* 'Rachelae', the latter collected by Professor Mahaffy in Greece in 1886. Alongside are drifts of winter aconites (*Eranthis hyemalis*), while in autumn these areas are covered with pink and white dwarf cyclamens.

Rockfield

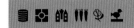

Location: Turn right at Lobinstown Cross off Ardee–Kells road, and after 3km
(2 miles) house is on far side of Julianstown Bridge on right

open: 2–6pm, by
appointment

Further information from:
Doyne and Georgina Nicholson,
Rockfield, Drumconrath, Navan,
Co Meath
Tel: 046 52135

Nearby sights of interest:
Francis Ledwidge Cottage Museum
(Slane): 17 Mar to Oct, daily,
10am–7pm (closes for lunch
1–2pm); Tel: 041 24244; Bend of
the Boyne Visitor Centre, Donore:
Apr to Feb, daily, 9.30am–5.30pm;
Tel: 041 24488.

This exceptionally pretty and unusual walled garden dates from
1784 and occupies 0.5ha (1 acre) below the house windows.
Uniquely, it slopes down on either side to a stream flowing
through the middle of the garden, which allows waterside
planting, while trees outside the walls help create a microclimate
for tender subjects such as abutilons, crinodendrons, and salvias.

The house passed to a great uncle of one of the present
owners in 1913, and after long neglect was revitalized in the 1930s
and improved by the present owners from 1965. From lawns
below the house, an axial path runs down the garden, crossing
the stream through dramatic box hedges. The stream banks are
planted with candelabra primulas, irises, hostas, astilbes, and
willow gentians, while the slopes above, divided by box-edged
paths, are filled with rows of vegetables, including sea kale and
globe artichokes. Tree peonies, lilacs, berberis, magnolias, pieris,
aralias, ceanothus, actinidias, and rambling roses, together with
numerous other shrubs and perennials, ooze from surrounding
borders, while a recently reconstructed glasshouse boasts
plumbagos, peaches, dianthus, and tender clematis varieties.

Astilbes, alchemillas, ferns, and
roses in an array of colour below
the glasshouse.

open: April to Oct, daily except Mon, 11am–5.30pm; all year for pre-booked groups

open: As above

Further information from:
John O'Driscoll, Head Gardener,
Strokestown Park, Strokestown,
Co Roscommon
Tel: 078 33013
Fax: 078 33712
e-mail: info@strokestownpark.ie

Nearby sights of interest:
Strokestown Famine Museum (in yards of house); King House, Boyle; Tel: 079 63242.

Vivid colours of *Astilbe* 'Fanal' and alstroemeria, backed by *Macleaya cordata* in the herbaceous border.

Strokestown Park

Location: Strokestown, on main Dublin–Sligo road (N5)

Strokestown is one of Ireland's finest Palladian houses and was the seat of the Pakenham Mahon family from the 1660s until 1979, when it was acquired by the Westward Group. Restoration of the 1740s house during the 1980s and the creation of a famine museum were followed in 1989 by plans to restore the 1.5ha (3½ acre) walled garden on the south side of the house and yards. Built in the 1740s, this garden remained in continuous use until the 1950s, when it was abandoned. Its transformation from field to garden took seven years, while in 2000 the 0.5ha (1.5 acre) slip garden was restored to its former magnificence.

The recreation of the main walled garden did not involve re-establishing the Edwardian garden exactly as it was, but rather utilizing relic features to produce a new garden. The old path layout was retained, as was the 18th-century pond, which was cleaned and filled with water lilies. The Long Border on the garden's north side was redesigned as a 150m (500ft) herbaceous border and its 5.5m (18ft) wide borders were filled to ensure an attractive and satisfying combination of colours from May to October. Other features include a croquet lawn overlooked by an Edwardian summerhouse, a "wild garden", a yew walk, and a rose garden overlooked by a stone pergola clad with *Clematis texensis* and *Schisandra rubriflora*.

The beautifully restored area outside the south side of the garden, known as the slip garden, was productive. It contains cold frames, a Regency melon house, an Edwardian tomato house and, in pride of place, a large, late 18th-century glasshouse and potting house range with reintroduced vines and peaches in the wings. The paths have been faithfully restored and the entire area replanted with herbs, vegetables, and cut flowers exactly as in its Edwardian heyday. A stunning view of the slip garden can be obtained from the recreated Palladian windows of the 1740s gazebo tower, now fully restored to its 18th-century condition.

32 *Talbot Botanic Gardens: Malahide Castle*

Location: 14.5km (9 miles) N of Dublin, outside Malahide

This irresistibly picturesque castle, partly medieval, gazes down on 6.5ha (16 acres) of shrubberies, which, together with a 1.5ha (4 acre) walled garden, contain one of the largest assemblages of non-ericaceous plants in the British Isles. The gardens were created by the late Lord Milo Talbot de Malahide from 1948 to 1973, and many of the 5,000 species and cultivars reflect his passion for southern-hemisphere plants, particularly from Tasmania and other parts of Australasia. Since 1976 the gardens have been superbly managed by Fingal County Council, which adds to the collections.

The shrubberies to the west and north of the castle are linked by lawns dominated by a Cedar of Lebanon. Among the shrubs, perennials, and carefully selected small trees are groups of escallonia, hebe, hypericum, ceanothus, crocosmia, eryngium, euphorbia, and pittosporum, while the scent of philadelphus, syringa, deutzia, and old roses fills the air. Many of Malahide's National Collection of *Olearia* are here, while others are in the Walled Garden, together with collections of honerias, melaleucas, callistemons, and climbers. The glasshouses hold many treasures, notably puyas, carmichaelias, lewisias, celmisias, and the rare *Paeonia cambessedesii*. Numerous alpines are kept in a small yard; more are near the Tresco Wall, itself festooned with tender climbers. The garden has a wonderful davidia, but the plant to note is *Garrya* 'Pat Ballard', which was propagated here.

open: May to Sep, daily, 2–4.30pm; guided tours of walled garden, Wed, 2pm

open: Apr to Oct, Mon to Sat, 10am–5pm, Sun and Public Holidays, 11am–6pm; Nov to Mar, Mon to Fri, 10am–5pm, Sat, Sun and Public Holidays, 2–5pm; closes for tours 12.45–2pm

Further information from:
Deniece Cranny, Fingal County Council, Malahide Castle, Malahide, Co Dublin
Tel: 01 8727777 or 8462184
Fax: 01 8727530 or 8462537
e-mail: malahidecastle@dublintourism.ie

Nearby sights of interest:
Newbridge Demesne; Tel: 01 436064; Newbridge House; Tel: 01 436534 or 01 727777 (Parks Dept); Lusk Heritage Centre: mid-Jun to mid-Sep, Fri, 9am–6pm; Tel: 01 8437683; Lusk Round Tower (keyholder: Mrs Kelly, Auto View, Dublin Road, Lusk).

The recently erected Victorian-style conservatory is a focal point.

33 *Tully: Japanese Gardens*

Location: 1.5km (1 mile) outside Kildare on Dublin road

open: 12 Feb to 12 Nov, Mon to Sat, 9.30-6pm, Sun, 2–5.50pm

Further information from:
The National Stud, Tully, Co Kildare
Tel: 045 521617 or 522963
Fax: 045 522964
e-mail: stud@irish-national-stud.ie
Website: www.irish-national-stud.ie

Nearby sights of interest:
The National Stud and Irish Horse Museum, Tully; Crookstown Mill, Ballitore: Apr to Sep, daily, 10am–7pm; Oct to Mar, 12 noon-5pm; Tel: 0507 23222.

The Bridge of Life crosses the stream below the Hill of Learning.

Tully is one of the best surviving products of the great vogue for Japanese-style gardens which followed the Anglo-Japanese Alliance of 1905. It was devised and subsequently presented to the state by Colonel Hall-Walker, later Baron Wavertree, whose boundless enthusiasm extended to importing a landscape designer, Tassa Eida, and his family from Japan, together with a shipload of plants, bonsai, stone ornaments, and even a teak geisha house. It was located next to his stud (now the National Stud) and was built between 1906 and 1910 by 40 labourers.

The garden symbolizes life's vicissitudes from the cradle to the grave. It incorporates great quantities of rock, a cave, blind paths, lawns, a tunnel, and a stream with bridges and lanterns. In addition to bonsai, the planting includes acers, cryptomerias, prunus, and bamboos, with a number of Japanese shrubs, such as *Broussonetia papyrifera* and *Hydrangea paniculata* 'Grandiflora'.

Entry tickets also permit access to the nearby St Fiachra's Garden, which resembles a golf course and has little to recommend it other than that it is a useful place for exercising one's dog.

Tullynally Castle

Location: 2.5km (1½ miles) outside Castlepollard on Granard road; signposted

The picturesque turrets of Tullynally Castle, one of Ireland's largest castellated houses, rise superbly in its magnificent 18th-century parkland setting. Among its many fine trees is a 250-year-old oak featured by the owner, Thomas Pakenham, in his acclaimed book *Meetings with Remarkable Trees*. There are lakes, one curved to resemble a river, an 18th-century grotto commanding wonderful views, and woodland walks through a wild garden with many trees and shrubs. In specially created clearings, some with focal features such as a rustic bower and a Chinese pavilion, the owner has planted many unusual plants collected on expeditions to China.

The walled garden, guarded by a pair of Coade-stone sphinxes, leads to a central walk of 200-year-old Irish yews, flanked by a rose walk, early Victorian glasshouses, lawns, and colourful herbaceous borders. More herbaceous borders lie outside the walled garden on a terrace around a summerhouse, amid lawns and informal planting of shrubs. Opposite lies a pond with a fascinating "weeping pillar", a type of fountain, dripping into a lily pond.

open: May to Aug, daily, 2–6pm

open: 15 Jun to 30 Jul and 12–27 Sep, 2.30–6pm; groups at other times by appointment

Further information from:
Valerie Pakenham, Tullynally Castle, Castlepollard, Co Westmeath
Tel: 044 61159
Fax: 044 61856

Nearby sights of interest:
Castlepollard Museum: all year, Sat and Sun, 2–6pm; Tel: 044 61168; ruins of Fore Abbey (keyholder: Peter Reilly, The Abbey House, Fore); Taghmon Church.

Herbaceous borders front the summerhouse outside the walled garden.

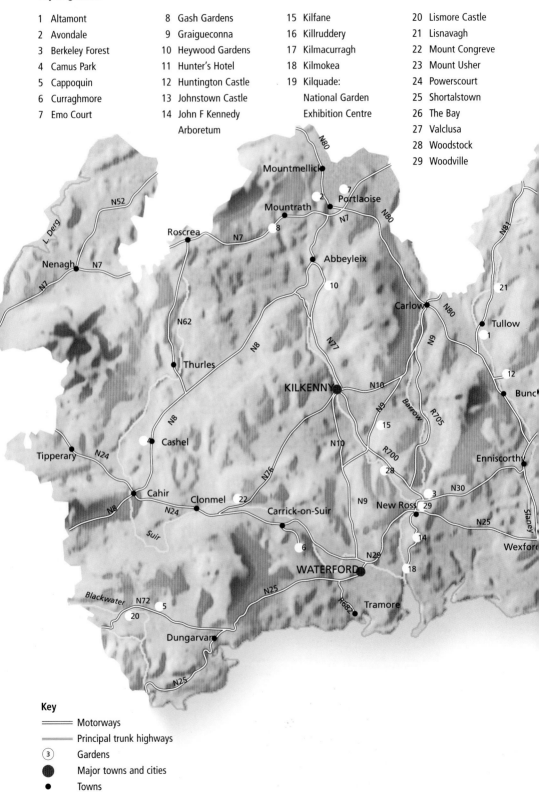

Key to gardens

1 Altamont	8 Gash Gardens	15 Kilfane	20 Lismore Castle
2 Avondale	9 Graigueconna	16 Killruddery	21 Lisnavagh
3 Berkeley Forest	10 Heywood Gardens	17 Kilmacurragh	22 Mount Congreve
4 Camus Park	11 Hunter's Hotel	18 Kilmokea	23 Mount Usher
5 Cappoquin	12 Huntington Castle	19 Kilquade:	24 Powerscourt
6 Curraghmore	13 Johnstown Castle	National Garden	25 Shortalstown
7 Emo Court	14 John F Kennedy	Exhibition Centre	26 The Bay
	Arboretum		27 Valclusa
			28 Woodstock
			29 Woodville

Key

═══ Motorways

─── Principal trunk highways

(3) Gardens

⬤ Major towns and cities

• Towns

South-eastern Ireland

Bray 9
24
27 16 R761
R755 N11
16
Greystones
Kilcoole
19
23
R752 11
Wicklow
15
2   17 N11
Arklow
Gorey

The eastern part of the ancient province of Munster and the southern half of Leinster make up the south-eastern region of this book. This encompasses some of the most fertile and picturesque parts of Ireland, with an annual rainfall of 75–125cm (30–50in), except on high ground, and mean temperatures of 5.5–6°C (42–3°F) in January to 15.5–16°C (60–61°F) in July. Historically, through its proximity to Great Britain, the region has been more exposed to invasion and outside influences than other parts of the country, which has contributed to a lively cultural diversity, reflected in its rich landscape heritage, its architecture, and its gardens.

Geographically, the region is dominated by the Leinster mountain chain, which extends south-west from Dublin Bay for over 120km (75 miles). This includes the great granite massif of the Wicklow Mountains,

Hardymount, County Carlow, one of many private gardens open during the Wicklow Gardens Festival.

Ireland's largest area of continuous upland, whose eastern
foothills have long been renowned for their lush, wooded
splendour and as the setting for numerous pretty villages,
demesnes, and gardens. In the 19th century, when
Dublin day trippers flocked to Powerscourt (see
pp.104–7) and other beauty spots, Wicklow became
known as the Garden of Ireland. Sadly, the area is being
rapidly submerged in commuter development, and even
the famous garden at Mount Usher (see pp.102–3), for
many the most exquisite in Ireland, is now overlooked by
a housing estate. Attempts locally to protect and promote
this garden heritage led to the establishment in 1989 of
the hugely successful Wicklow Gardens Festival. This
takes place every May and June and, in addition to
hosting gardening day schools, flowering arranging, and
other events, it facilitates the opening of numerous high-
quality private gardens that are not normally accessible
to the public. Brochures can be obtained from Wicklow
County Tourism by telephoning 0404 200100 or
e-mailing wctr@iol.ie

The counties of Kilkenny, Carlow, and Wexford,
together with the two Munster counties of Tipperary
and Waterford, consist largely of attractive rolling
countryside, broken by a number of small hill ranges
and the picturesque river valleys of the "three sisters", the
Suir, Nore, and Barrow. Amid this lush countryside are
some fine gardens, notably Heywood (see p.90), Kilfane
(see p.94), and Woodstock (see p.110), though the largest
and finest are Mount Congreve (see pp.100–1) and
Altamont (see pp.82–3). Undeniably, many of the area's
best gardens, including Shortalstown (see p.108),
Woodville (see p.111), and Kilmokea (see p.97), lie in
the coastal band of the fertile, arable county of Wexford,
all taking advantage of an exceptionally mild, almost
subtropical climate.

**Lawns flowing around generously
planted mixed borders at The
Bay, County Wexford.**

 Altamont

open: Mon to Fri, 9am–5pm, and some weekends

Location: 8km (5 miles) from Tullow; signposted off N80 and N81 between Tullow and Bunclody

Further information from:
The Manager, Pauline Dowling,
Dúchas – The Heritage Service,
Altamont, Tullow, Co Carlow
Tel: 0503 59444; also 0503 59128
for Paul Cuttler, head gardener

Nearby sights of interest:
Pleasant walk up Mount Leinster,
outside Myshall, on a clear day.

Altamont is a delightfully enchanting place that exudes memories of the late Corona North, whose skilled and artistic planting made this one of the great garden pleasures of Ireland. Combining formal areas around the house with informal and wild parts beyond, the 16ha (40 acre) garden incorporates a lake, an arboretum, a romantic riverside walk, a splendid herbaceous border, and much more. Visitors should allow themselves plenty of time to explore.

Although the house and surrounding parkland belong largely to the 1770s, the garden assumed much of its present appearance during the 1840s, when a lake of 1ha (2½ acres) was dug, and terraced lawns were created below the house. After the property was acquired in the early 20th century by Feilding Lecky Watson, the garden was filled with rare trees and shrubs, many obtained through his joint sponsorship of Himalayan expeditions. His death in 1943 was followed by a period of decline for the garden, until from the 1970s it was restored and expanded by his daughter, Corona North. She died in 1999, leaving Altamont to the state, which now manages it through Dúchas – the Heritage Service.

The garden is entered through a small gate onto a walk of 18th-century beeches known as the Nun's Walk. A path leads to the house, where a pond is flanked by a fine collection of dwarf conifers and shrubs. Opposite, a bed is filled with choice plants,

Lakeside planting in a view towards the island.

such as golden bays (*Laurus nobilis* 'Aurea'), the dogwood *Cornus alterifolia* 'Argentea', and the tree peony *Paeonia lutea* var. *ludlowii*. The walk to the lake has box-hedged rose beds with many lovely old varieties, such as the pink *R.* 'Céleste'. Across sweeping lawns is a fine collection of trees and shrubs, while the lake margins proffer many moisture-loving plants, including a good selection of hostas, astilbes, gunneras, candelabra primulas, and meconopsis. A stone bridge, completed in 1997, leads along the opposite shore to an arboretum and a bog garden and through ancient oak woods to the River Slaney Walk. The old granite "100 Steps" lead visitors back up, past a little temple. The climax of the visit is the magnificent double herbaceous border in the walled garden, designed by Assumpta Broomfield and completed in 2000 as a fitting tribute to the late Corona North.

An exquisite spring scene of wild daffodils on the steps leading down to the River Slaney Walk.

open: All year, daily,
10am–1pm and 2–6pm
open: Mar to Oct, 11am–6pm

Further information from:
The Manager
Tel: 0404 46111

Nearby sights of interest:
Greenan Farm Museums and
Maze, Ballinanty: May to Sep, Tue
to Sun, 10am–6.30pm; Tel: 0404
36308.

 ## *Avondale*

Location: 1.5km (1 mile) S of Rathdrum; signposted

The Irish parliamentarian Charles Stewart Parnell (1846–91)
lived here and his life is celebrated by an exhibition in the
mansion. Avondale played a major role in the history of Irish
forestry and its demesne is now a forest park. Planting was begun in
the 1770s by Samuel Hayes, and in 1904, after it became a forestry
school, experimental plots were laid down with advice from the
plant collector Augustine Henry, who is commemorated with a
grove of his introductions. Among Avondale's best trees are a large
Cupressus arizonica, two high silver firs near the lower path, and a
fine *Chamaecyparis lawsoniana* 'Wisselli' in front of the house.

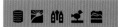

open: May to Sep, Thu and
Fri; Sat and Sun, by appointment

Further information from:
Countess Anne Bernstorff, Berkeley
Forest, New Ross, Co Wexford
Tel: 051 21361

Nearby sights of interest:
Costume collection in main house.

**Grassy terraces lead up to the
thatched summerhouse.**

 ## *Berkeley Forest*

Location: 6.5km (4 miles) from New Ross, on minor road (near golf course) off main
Enniscorthy road

The beguiling, ochre-coloured house, set in lovely parkland with
views of the distant Blackstairs Mountains, was named in honour
of the Irish Anglican bishop and philosopher George Berkeley
(1685–1753). It is flanked by an old walled garden on sloping
ground, 0.2ha (½ acre) of which was remodelled in the 1960s by
Countess Anne and the late Count Gunnar Bernstorff. They
created a series of terraces culminating in a charming thatched
summerhouse, dated 1815, which they had rescued from the
grounds of a Carmelite convent in New Ross.

  The garden's planting is unusual in that the colour schemes
have been controlled by the painter
Anne Bernstorff to allow blue,
silver, and grey to dominate. There
are clumps of *Ceanothus impressus*,
masses of delphiniums and banks
of hydrangeas. Gentians, violas,
forget-me-nots, lithospermums,
bellflowers, and hostas are used
extensively, as is the silver foliage
of *Artemisia arborescens*, lamb's ears,
and purple sage. Tall conifers,
such as *Chamaecyparis lawsoniana*
'Columnaris', give the garden
height, while dwarf conifers, such
as *Chamaecyparis pisifera* 'Plumosa',
provide body and texture.

Camus Park

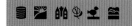

Location: S end of Cashel (at T-junction at bottom of square). Turn right on to Dundrum road and take second big house gate on left, marked "Camus Park Stud"

This lush and stylish garden was created during the 1990s around the home of the Hyde family, who are well known in the world of Irish racing. It spreads out over 1.2ha (3 acres), encompassing a series of separate areas on different levels. A mood of formality greets visitors along an avenue flanked with clipped laurel hedging and protruding stands of whitebeam and Himalayan birch. In front of the house a level lawn falls down to a Robinsonian wild garden, where a pool, enclosed by sheltering trees, plays host to naturalized ferns, grasses, hemerocallis, anemones, hellebores, and candelabra primulas. On the opposite side, by contrast, sweeping lawns flow around deep, curving beds of herbaceous perennials. At the back these borders drift around a short flight of steps, which leads through a wrought-iron gate to a sheltered courtyard paved in gravel and Liscannor flagstones. In the centre stand columnar Irish yews and topiary in terracotta pots, while the perimeter walls support climbers and shrubs at home in a Mediterranean climate, such as *Passiflora caerulea*, the yellow-flowering *Bupleurum fruticosum*, and the lemon-scented verbena. There is also a pergola cloaked in wisteria and a collection of alpines, some in old stone troughs.

open: Groups only, by appointment, 2–6pm

Further information from:
Mrs Trish Hyde, Camus Park,
Co Tipperary
Tel: 062 61010

Nearby sights of interest:
Rock of Cashel: opening times vary; Tel: 062 61437.

A verdant water garden lies below the house.

Cappoquin

Location: Just NE of Cappoquin on Dungarvan road (N72)

open: Apr to Jul, Mon to Sat, 9am–1pm; closes Sun and Bank Holidays

open: As above

Further information from:
Sir Richard and Lady Keane,
Cappoquin House, Cappoquin,
Co Waterford
Tel: 058 54004 or 54073
Fax: 058 54698
Peter Stam in the Walled Garden
Tel: 058 54787
Fax: 058 52083

Cappoquin House is a handsome ashlar pile of the 1770s set in a scenic location above the Blackwater valley. Elegant parkland sweeps south down to the village, while the slopes above are occupied by a 1.2ha (3 acre) pleasure garden. This has a Victorian origin, but owes its current distinction to the present Lady Keane, who has gardened here since the 1940s.

Lady Keane's planting skills are immediately apparent in the courtyard, where a corner has been transformed into a delightful cottage garden. The pleasure garden, which overhangs the courtyard, is divided into terraced areas, each with sweeping lawns flowing around irregular beds containing a mixture of trees, shrubs, and perennials. The shrubs have been carefully chosen for their soft colours, scent, open habit, and ability to flourish in the garden's quite exposed position. Old rose varieties play an

Colourful borders flank the lawn.

important role, but rhododendrons are dominant and include the white, scented hybrid 'Lady Alice Fitzwilliam', the magnificent 'Cornish Cross', with its delicious tones of pink, species and hybrids of *R. griersonianum*, and that great Irish favourite *R. augustinii*. Some impressive old trees and an enormous *Rhododendron arboreum* hide the old Walled Garden, where Peter Stam has a bamboo nursery.

Curraghmore

Location: 22.5km (14 miles) from Waterford. Entrance to east of Portlaw village

open: Easter to Oct, Thu afternoons and Bank Holidays

Further information from:
The Marquess of Waterford,
Curraghmore, Portlaw,
Co Waterford
Tel: 051 387102
Fax: 051 38748

Nearby sights of interest:
French Church and Waterford
Heritage Centre, Waterford.

A vast mid-18th-century forecourt, recalling the splendours of a Continental palace, leads to this fine mansion, which commands views of a demesne unsurpassed in Ireland. It has many fine trees, including the tallest in Ireland, a Sitka spruce 56m (185ft) high. The gardens, laid out by Fraser in 1843, resemble Le Nôtre's garden at Rambouillet. They include a formal semicircular balustrade from which radiates a *patte-d'oie* of three avenues. *Bosquets* formed in the flanking woods have many delightful clearings, in one of which stands the famous shell house of c1755, containing a statue by the younger John van Nost of Lady Catherine Power, who put up the shells with her own hand.

Emo Court

Location: Between Portlaoise (Maryborough) and Monasterevin, 1.5km (1 mile) N of N7 at New Inn

The focus of the gardens is a monumental neoclassical house by the celebrated Irish architect James Gandon, built in the 1790s for the first Earl of Portarlington. Having served as a Jesuit novitiate for many years, the house was restored in the 1970s by Mr Cholmeley-Harrison, who has since given the property and its 22ha (55 acres) of extensively improved gardens to the state.

The sweeping lawns north and east of the house are criss-crossed by avenues of dignified Florence Court yews planted in Victorian times, with statues of the Four Seasons. To the west lies a woodland garden, the Clucker, containing some of the garden's finest trees, including large examples of *Cedrus deodara*, *Pinus radiata*, and *Picea smithiana*. Beneath the canopy is a wide selection of shrubs, notably azaleas, rhododendrons, camellias, and pieris, with some striking Japanese maples, the spice-scented *Cornus nuttallii*, and calico bushes (*Kalmia latifolia*). More maples line the route to the Grapery, north-east of the house, where an attractive arboretum is crossed by walks with evocative names such as the Via Davidia and the Apiary Walk. A recently restored lake of 10.5ha (26 acres) lies to the north and beyond, on a distant hill, stands an impressive 18th-century folly.

open: Jul to Aug, daylight hours; guided tours every Sun, 3pm, or by prior arrangement

open: Mid-Jun to mid-Sep; guided tours of house, 10.30am–5pm; last tour 4.30pm

Further information from:
Mavis Duggan, Dúchas – The Heritage Service, Emo Court, Co Leix
Tel: 0502 26573

Nearby sights of interest:
Coolbanagher Church by James Gandon (1785).

An attractive vista from the arboretum to the house.

Gash Gardens

Location: 800m (½ mile) off main Dublin–Limerick road at Castletown, S of Mountrath; signposted

open: May to Sep, Mon to Sat, 10am–5pm, Sun, 2–5pm; other times by arrangement; no children or dogs; not suitable for wheelchairs

Further information from:
Mary Keenan, Gash, Castletown, Co Leix
Tel: 0502 32247
Fax: 0502 32857

Nearby sights of interest:
Slieve Bloom Environmental Park.

You would not expect to find such a place down a midlands country road, and even when you arrive there is nothing to indicate the exceptional garden and nursery that lie behind the modest wooden gates. It was started in 1984 when a dairy farmer, the late Noel Keenan, gave up his milk round to devote himself to a lifelong passion for gardening. When he died in March 2000 he left a garden of 1.5ha (4 acres) that extends in a long strip from his house down to the banks of the River Nore.

Curiously, the earliest parts of the garden lie at the greatest distance from the house. The riverside walk is approached down a beech walk 180m (600ft) long and entered through a laburnum arch. On the way down visitors can admire long herbaceous borders and a collection of trees and shrubs set in extensive lawns. There is a stream garden, with gunneras, hostas, and ligularias and a special area for growing ferns. Nearest to the house is an extensive rock garden boasting colourful herbaceous perennials and many rare alpines, focused on a "moonhouse" grotto, a small cascade, and a lily pond. A summerhouse and seats offer good vantage points over this attractive garden.

View across the rock garden and "moonhouse" grotto with landscape beyond.

Graigueconna

Location: Last house on left in Old Connaught Avenue from Bray, opposite a grass traffic island

Although the bones of this 1.5ha (3½ acres) garden were devised by Lewis Meredith, the celebrated Edwardian alpine enthusiast, the present garden is very much the creation of his granddaughter, Rosemary Brown, who inherited the property in 1970 after it had suffered years of neglect. Her garden is renowned for the variety of its plants and their skilful combination.

The layout is given a formal axis by a grassy walk flanked by Irish yews, which is lined with a wonderful admixture of largely pale-coloured herbaceous perennials, shrubs – including striking evergreens, such as melianthus and spiky or grassy plant clumps, such as sisyrinchium and foxtail rush. Mixed borders adjacent to the house have plants with hotter colours, while beyond the kitchen garden a rose border contains numerous varieties of old-fashioned cultivars. Many more roses lie in the old orchard, including *Rosa multiflora* clambering through the old trees. At the top of the garden the enormous rockery is planted with hellebores, ferns, aroids, small beds of primulas, and exotics such as *Dryas octopetala* and *Celmisia*. There is a fine strawberry tree and a variegated hellebore now registered as 'Graigueconna'.

open: May to Jul, by appointment to groups of four or more

Further information from:
Mrs Rosemary Brown, Graigueconna, Old Connaught Avenue, Bray, Co Wicklow
Tel: 01 282 2273

Nearby sights of interest:
Powerscourt house, gardens, and waterfall (see pp.104–7); Dargle Glen.

The centre walk, flanked by clipped Irish yews and mixed borders.

Heywood Gardens

open: Jul to Aug, daylight
hours; guided tours every Sun at
3pm, or by prior appointment

Further information from:
Pat Shortis, Dúchas – The Heritage
Service, Heywood, Ballinakill,
Co Leix
Tel: 0502 33563 or 056 51863

Nearby sights of interest:
Durrow Abbey's 10th-century
High Cross.

Location: 8km (5 miles) SE of Abbeyleix on N side of Ballinakill village

This was one of the very few gardens in Ireland created by the famous partnership of Edwin Lutyens and Gertrude Jekyll. Built for Colonel Hutchinson Poë in 1909–12, it comprised a series of three separate gardens linked by a terrace fronting a great mansion. The mansion is now gone, having burnt down in 1950, but from 1985 a programme of restoration was begun on the gardens, with planting plans supplied by Graham Stuart Thomas to augment the lost 1910 Jekyll designs.

From a series of small compartments bounded by clipped yew hedges, visitors descend a curving staircase into an elliptical garden where three terraced borders drop to a central oval pond encircling a fountain. At the east end stands a pavilion with a steep pantile roof, while at the opposite end an elegant wrought-iron gate leads down an *allée* of pleached limes to a flat terrace lawn with herbaceous borders. Beyond is a pergola terrace whose oak beams support Ionic columns that once belonged to the gallery in the Irish House of Commons. From here there are dramatic views over an elegant landscape park laid out in the 1770s in the romantic-poetic tradition.

The pond and its metal tortoises in the terraced elliptical garden.

Hunter's Hotel

Location: 2.5km (1½ miles) after left turn at bridge at Ashford on N11 from Dublin

open: All year

In an unspoiled part of Wicklow, this is an old coaching inn which has had an attractive garden for over a century. Some early plantings still survive, including an old yew by the waters of the River Vartry. Amid the garden's box-edged beds and lawns there are some striking trees and shrubs, such as a paulownia with foxglove-shaped flowers, stately cordylines, a ginkgo, yellow-flowering fremontodendrons, a tulip tree, a podocarpus, a southern beech, magnolias, and rhododendrons. The garden boasts colourful displays of roses and herbaceous perennials, and is noted for its oriental poppies in spring.

Further information from:
Mr Gilletlie, Hunter's Hotel,
Newrath Bridge, Rathnew,
Co Wicklow
Tel: 0404 40106
Fax: 0404 40338
e-mail: reception@hunters.ie

Nearby sights of interest:
South Wicklow; Mount Usher
gardens (see pp.102–3).

Huntington Castle

Location: Clonegal village

open: Sun afternoon and by appointment
open: As above

Huntington is an irresistible castellated house with an atmosphere of quiet antiquity and charm. The stronghouse of 1625–30 was substantially remodelled in the 1670s by Sir Lawrence Esmonde and it was during this time that many of Huntington's garden features originated. A straight lime avenue was planted from the village and long canals were dug both above and below the castle. The most significant survival, however, and the feature for which Huntington is famous, is the rows of English yew. In the 17th century these formed part of a hedge, probably around the original gardens, but they have now attained a considerable size and are one of the arboreal sights of Ireland.

Further information from:
Mrs Moira Robertson, Huntington
Castle, Clonegal, Co Carlow
Tel: 054 77552

Nearby sights of interest:
Bunclody, a centre for hillwalking
in the Blackstairs Mountains.

Steps to the 1890s conservatory
on the garden front.

Italianate gardens were laid down on the south side of the castle during the 1860s, when Alexander Durdin was remodelling the house. Only recently restored, these comprise terraced lawns with a fountain, a summerhouse, and rows of Irish yews, overlooked by an Edwardian conservatory. There is an arboretum on the ground below, which falls to a lake, where an 1880s water-turbine house is a focal point. Beyond, there are fine walks through park woodland in this idyllic countryside.

open: All year, daily,
9.30am–5pm

Further information from:
Teagasc (Food and Agriculture
Authority), Johnstown Castle,
Murrintown, Co Wexford
Tel: 053 42888

Nearby sights of interest:
Irish Agricultural Museum,
Johnstown: Jun to Aug, Mon to Fri,
9am–5pm, Sat and Sun, 2–5pm;
Apr, May and Sep, Mon to Fri,
9am–5pm, Sat and Sun, 2–5pm;
Tel: 053 42888 or 42004;
Rathmacknee Castle (keyholder:
Patrick Kavanagh, Rathmacknee);
National Heritage Park, Ferrycarrig:
Mar to Oct, 10am–7pm; Apr to Sep,
9.30am–6.30pm; Tel: 053 41733.

View from the statue terrace
across the lake to the castle.

13 *Johnstown Castle*

Location: On Rosslare road from Wexford, take first turn on right; signposted

The castle is a magnificent Gothic-revival extravaganza of silvery-grey ashlar set in a ornamental demesne of lakes, woodlands, lush lawns, and gardens. It was built for the Grogan-Morgan family between 1810 and 1855, while the grounds were largely laid out in the 1830s by Daniel Robertson, and included a 2ha (5 acre) lake fronting the castle terraces, a Gothic "fishing tower", and a walk lined with classical statuary on the opposite bank. Robertson's airy, Italianate splendours are complemented by many fine trees and shrubs in the vicinity of the castle, including a fine example of *Cryptomeria japonica* 'Elegans', a range of false cypresses, rare oaks such as the Makimo oak and *Quercus* x *pseudoturneri*, large redwoods, and some of the oldest specimens of Monterey cypress in Ireland.

The woodland garden, to the west of the castle lake, is focused on the ruins of the medieval castle of Rathlannon. In the glades here grow fine magnolias, viburnums, dogwoods, and some striking fern-leafed beeches (*Fagus sylvatica* 'Aspleniifolia'). Nearby is a 0.8ha (2 acre) lake, dug in the 1860s, and the walled garden, now rehabilitated. Its glasshouses have been replaced by a large, modern plant house, but the garden's main feature is a long and grandiose gravel path dividing herbaceous borders and backed by clipped yew hedges.

Johnstown Castle was gifted to the nation in 1945 and has been home to an agricultural institute for many years.

John F Kennedy Arboretum

Location: 11km (7 miles) S of New Ross. From Wexford road (N26) take Campile road (R733); signposted to left off Wexford–Waterford road (N25), just S of New Ross and R733

This is a young arboretum planted on a vast scale. Established on the slopes overlooking John F Kennedy's ancestral home, it embraces 250ha (625 acres) and contains 4,500 species of trees and shrubs. The planting was carried out between 1964 and 1968 by the Forest and Wildlife Service and was transferred to the Office of Public Works in 1994.

The collection is laid out in botanical sequence, with three well-labelled examples of every species represented. There are two circuits, one of gymnospermae (conifers) and the other of angiospermae (broadleaves), and these are interwoven to provide colour throughout the year. The collections of eucalyptus, poplars, magnolias, maples, and cherries are impressive, as is the Ericaceous Garden, which contains an enormous variety of heathers, pieris, and other peat-loving plants, including over 500 rhododendrons. There is a Phenological Garden exploring the relationship between climate and biological phenomena, a lake with waterside planting, and a 0.4ha (1 acre) alpine garden with a mixture of over 320 varieties of dwarf and slow-growing conifers. Any remaining energy might be reserved for a trip to the summit of Slievecoiltia, which offers a magnificent panorama of the whole arboretum.

open: May to Aug, daily, 10am–8pm; Apr and Sep, daily, 10am–6.30pm; Oct to Mar, daily, 10am–5pm

Further information from:
Christopher Kelly, Dúchas – The Heritage Service, John F Kennedy Arboretum, New Ross, Co Wexford
Tel: 051 388171
Fax: 051 388172

Nearby sights of interest:
Dunbrody Abbey and Visitors Centre, Campile: Apr to Sep, daily, 10am–6pm; Tel: 051 88603; Tintern Abbey: contact Gerry Cruise Jnr; Tel: 051 62281.

Part of the large alpine garden, which contains a wide variety of dwarf and slow-growing conifers.

93

15 *Kilfane*

Location: 3km (2 miles) N of Thomastown; signposted on Dublin road

open: Apr to last week Sep, Sun, 2–6pm; Jul and Aug, daily, 11am–6pm; groups by appointment at other times

Further information from:
Mrs Susan Mosse, Kilfane, Thomastown, Co Kilkenny
Tel: 056 24558
Fax: 056 27491
Website: www.nicholasmosse.com

Nearby sights of interest:
Jerpoint Abbey, one of Ireland's finest Cistercian abbey ruins: St Patrick's weekend, 10am–5pm; Easter weekend, 10am–5pm; mid-Apr to mid-Jun, daily except Mon, 10am–5pm; mid-Jun to end Sep, daily, 9.30am–6.30pm; end Sep to mid-Oct, daily, 10am–5pm; Tel: 056 24623.

Springtime view of the stream and *cottage orné* in Kilfane glen.

The secluded wooded glen at Kilfane, with its delightfully romantic *cottage orné* and cascade, is an outstanding manifestation of the late 18th-century love for rugged, picturesque beauty. Originally part of the demesne of Kilfane House, some 3km (2 miles) distant, this 24ha (60 acre) glen was designed to utilize its inherent natural features to create variety and surprise. Winding paths, rocky eminences, woodland clearings, a rustic bridge, and other dramatic incidents all feature on the journey down to the deep valley bottom, where visitors are greeted by a surreal scene that could be out of a fairy tale by the Brothers Grimm. A *cottage orné* with thick thatch and diamond trellis-work entwined with clematis, honeysuckle, and jasmine overlooks a smooth lawn broken by a stream. Opposite there is a 9m (30ft) high artificial waterfall cascading into a pool and, nearby, a hermit's grotto.

Cottages ornés were commonly used for entertaining in Regency times and it is tantalizing to imagine that the poet Thomas Moore, a friend of the Power family of Kilfane, must have come here. The cottage was long gone when Nicholas and Susan Mosse acquired the property in the 1980s. Using old illustrations and evidence on the ground, they reconstructed the cottage, the waterfall, and the setting, having cleared the glen of dense undergrowth. By their home above the glen they have also created an attractive, compartmentalized garden which includes herbaceous borders and a "moongarden" filled with white flowers.

16 *Killruddery*

Location: Off link road from N11 (Bray and Greystones exit)

The gardens at Killruddery were begun in 1682 by Captain Edward Brabazon, the fourth Earl of Meath, and later extended by his nephew, the sixth earl, in the 1720s. Much of their original formal layout still survives; indeed, Killruddery must be counted the most complete example of a garden of the late 17th or early 18th century to survive in the British Isles

Typically for the period, the gardens were arranged axially upon the house, though the central feature of two parallel canals leading to a circular pond has parallels on the Continent rather than in Ireland. These canals, each 170m (550ft) long, extend down a rectangular lawn, aligned upon a double lime avenue running 800m (½ mile) uphill across the deer park. The circular pond boasts a fountain and beyond lies a series of restored water cascades. Flanking the east side of the canal lawn is the Angles, a *bosquet* in the form of a St Andrew's cross. Once a standard feature of Irish gardens of this period, it comprises tall, radiating hedges with statuary at the intersections. A combination of lime, hornbeam, yew, and beech has been used in these hedges, which are clipped once a year, in winter. West of the canal lawn lies the Wilderness, a beech wood divided by symmetrical walks with statues placed at focal points. This leads to a circular pond framed by a double beech hedge with Barbezat's fountain of children at play in the centre. Nearby is the remarkable Sylvan Theatre, used for amateur theatricals, with its grassy amphitheatre seats, and bay hedge surround.

In the 1820s Killruddery House was remodelled and enlarged in the Tudor-revival style, and in 1846 stone balustrading and a floral parterre were added to the west front. This side of the house is overlooked by an ornamental dairy designed by Sir George Hodson and by a conservatory, the work of the Scottish architect William Burn, with a domed roof by Richard Turner.

open: Apr to Sep, daily, 1–5pm; groups by appointment at other times

open: May, Jun and Sep, daily, 1–5pm; groups by appointment at other times

Further information from:
Ailbhe de Buitléar, Killruddery, Bray, Co Wicklow
Tel: 01 286 2777 or 286 3405
Fax: 01 286 2777

Nearby sights of interest:
Agricultural Heritage Display, Coolakay House, Enniskerry:
Apr to Oct, daily, 10am–6pm;
Tel: 01 286 2423.

The west end of the statue gallery in the recently restored domed conservatory designed in 1852 by William Burn.

 ### *Kilmacurragh*

open: All year, daily

Location: Turn left at Tap pub 8km (5 miles) S of Rathnew and again at T-junction 2.5km (1½ miles) further on; gates 450m (500 yards) on left

Further information from:
The Manager, Kilmacurragh,
Dúchas – The Heritage Service
Tel: 01 661 3111

Nearby sights of interest:
Avondale; the meeting of the waters at Avoca.

For years this remarkable arboretum, now in the process of conservation, has tottered on the brink of extinction. It is dominated by conifers and calcifuges planted by Thomas Acton (1826–1908) in the grounds of his home, built in 1697. From the early 1850s he cultivated vast numbers of tender species, and although his planting was Robinsonian in style, he kept the bones of the original formal layout, the vistas and avenues of which are still focused on the house, now ruined. A striking feature from the 1690s is the former yew hedges flanking a pond below the house.

The arboretum is famous for its rhododendrons. Amid vast *Rhododendron arboreum* there are striking examples of red-flowering *R. roylei*, *R. davidsonianum*, *R. thomsonii*, *R. augustinii*, and sweetly scented *R. griffithianum*. Among the many exceptional trees are a *Saxegothaea conspicua*; *Cryptomeria japonica* 'Elegans' and *Podocarpus salignus* in front of the house; a *Cupressus cashmeriana*, a *Laurelia serrata*, and a tall *Fitzroya cupressoides*. In the walled garden are a *Nothofagus moorei* planted in 1887, a spectacular *Embothrium coccineum*, and an enormous *Magnolia campbellii*. Sadly, the original of *Chamaecyparis lawsoniana* 'Kilmacurragh', a slender form of Lawson's cypress, no longer survives.

Carpets of crimson petals on a path overhung by towering arboreum rhododendrons.

Kilmokea

Location: From New Ross, take the R733, signposted for Campile and the John F Kennedy Arboretum; before Campile turn right for Great Island

Topiary work in yew, an endless variety of hedging and an exceptional range of plants are features of this exquisite subtropical garden in the grounds of a Georgian rectory. Started in 1946 by the late Colonel David Price and his wife Joan, it covers 3ha (8 acres) and takes full advantage of a mild microclimate.

The area around the house was designed to be formal and compartmentalized, incorporating attractive walling, pathways, hedging, and an old dovecote. A focal point is a pedimented loggia, which overlooks a paved lily pool fringed with a glorious mixture of roses, verbascums, acanthus, dicentras, and self-seeding valerians beneath a large *Magnolia* x *soulangeana*. Behind the house extend open lawns flanked by a lupin border and an iris garden opposite curving herbaceous borders, which lead the eye down to a gateway bordered by rose beds. Beyond lies a tropical garden and across the road a woodland garden, remarkably well developed considering that it was begun from scratch in 1968. Here, along winding paths and around two ponds, are mounds of hydrangeas, azaleas, large numbers of acers, myrtles, magnolias, and at least 50 camellia cultivars. The ponds play host to skunk cabbages, rodgersias, hostas, and other moisture-loving plants.

open: Mar to Nov, daily, 10am–5pm

Further information from:
Mark and Emma Hewlett,
Kilmokea, Great Island, Campile,
Co Wexford
Tel: 051 388109
Fax: 051 388776
e-mail: kilmokea@indigo.ie
Website: www.kilmokea.com

Nearby sights of interest:
John F Kennedy Arboretum
(see p.93).

The loggia with lily pond fringed by *Alchemilla mollis, Dierama pulcherrimum*, and valerian.

19 *Kilquade: National Garden Exhibition Centre*

Location: S of Glen of the Downs, on a minor road off N11

open: Mon to Sat, 10am–6pm, Sun, 1–6pm; no dogs

Further information from:
Tim and Suzanne Wallis, Kilquade, Co Wicklow
Tel: 01 281 9890
Fax: 01 281 0359
e-mail: calumet@clubi.ie
Website: www.clubi.ie/calumet

Nearby sights of interest:
Glen of the Downs Nature Reserve; Avoca Handweavers: all year, daily, 9.30am–6pm; Tel: 0402 35105.

The placing of nurseries beside gardens open to the public has become commonplace in recent years, but at Kilquade the process is reversed. Here a series of gardens has been specially designed so that nursery visitors can see the plants *in situ*. Started in 1993, the centre now covers 1ha (3 acres) and embraces 18 model gardens by leading designers. Linked by the Harlequin Walk, brilliantly coloured with summer bedding, these include an acid garden, a river garden, and a town garden, and all have matured well. The gardens are beautifully maintained and benefit from labelling which is discreet but comprehensive.

20 *Lismore Castle*

Location: Lismore

open: 22 Apr to 15 Oct, daily, 1.45–4.45pm

Further information from:
Michael Penruddock, Lismore Castle, Lismore, Co Waterford
Tel: 058 54424
Fax: 058 54896

Nearby sights of interest:
St Carthage's Cathedral, Lismore.

Lismore boasts a remarkable example of an early 17th-century defended garden, which has remained continuously in use to this day. Built in 1626 by Richard Boyle, the Great Earl of Cork, this 1ha (3 acre) enclosure, known as the Upper Garden, lies adjacent to the honey-tinted walls of the romantic castle and is enclosed by high walls with turrets. It contains a raised walk with topiary at one end and falls in a series of terraces, divided centrally by a path aligned on the town's medieval cathedral. Today this central walk is flanked by colourful herbaceous borders backed by clipped yew hedges, while behind lie an orchard, extensive lawns, and flowerbeds. In the north-west

The Upper Garden in spring, looking towards the castle.

corner stands a ridge-and-furrow glasshouse designed in 1858 by Joseph Paxton for the sixth Duke of Devonshire, whose family had inherited the property through marriage in 1748.

Entry to the Upper Garden is through the Riding House, which was erected in 1631 to provide accommodation for mounted horsemen. This building also gives access to the Victorian pleasure ground, known as the Lower Garden, which was created c1850 by the bachelor duke. Here there is a colourful display of spring-flowering shrubs, notably camellias, magnolias, cherries, azaleas, and rhododendrons. The principal feature is an ancient yew walk, said to have been planted in 1707.

Lisnavagh

Location: SE of Rathvilly. From Hacketstown, take Carlow road (R727) and turn right at Tobinstown; entrance is on left

open: May to Jul, Sun, 2–6pm and by appointment; no dogs

Further information from:
Lady Jessica Rathdonnell,
Lisnavagh, Co Carlow
Tel: 0503 61104
Fax: 0503 61148

This Tudor-revival house is set in sweeping, velvety lawns that seamlessly extend into a panorama of distant mountains. On one side a line of yews screens the pleasure ground designed by Daniel Robertson after 1847. The maintained gardens were much reduced after the house was rebuilt in 1953, but from the 1980s they have been reclaimed, with new features added, and now total 4ha (10 acres).

The manor house looms from behind a large herbaceous border.

The path into the pleasure ground is fringed with shrubs beneath a canopy of trees. The extensive arboretum beyond, criss-crossed by cathedral-like walks of Irish yews, has an array of rhododendrons, camellias, eucryphias, embothriums, and other shrubs. Close to the house an L-shaped herbaceous border is filled with perennials, while more displays lie in an enclosed garden that flanks the walled garden. In addition to a swimming pool, this area boasts an alpine rockery and a lily pond enclosed by a jungle-like profusion of water-loving plants.

Further information from:
The Estate Office, Mount
Congreve, Kilmeaden, Co
Waterford
Tel: 051 384115
Fax: 051 384576

Nearby sights of interest:
Touraneena Heritage Farm,
Ballinamult; Tel: 058 47353.

In spring the dazzling colours,
particularly of the azaleas, can
be at times overpowering.

Mount Congreve

Location: 8km (5 miles) from Waterford, off Waterford–Cork road at Kilmeaden

The sheer magnitude of Mount Congreve can be difficult to grasp, let alone describe. Covering 47ha (115 acres) with 18km (11¼ miles) of paths, these gardens contain an astonishing 9,000 varieties of rare trees and shrubs, representing over 250,000 plants in what must be one of the most comprehensive collections of its kind in the world.

Most of the gardens enjoy an informal setting beneath a canopy of oak around a large, 18th-century mansion on the banks of the River Suir. Begun in 1963, the planting has concentrated on flowering trees and shrubs, though Mr Congreve endeavoured to grow every plant that will thrive here. Under the direction of his head gardener, Mr Dool, these were planted in positions most advantageous to their growth and aesthetic appeal. The varieties

were never planted singly, but in groups of six or more; in some cases there are over 100 examples of one variety. This idea of group planting for bold effect, one of the great hallmarks of Mount Congreve, was inspired by Lionel de Rothschild's garden at Exbury, in Hampshire, England, which Mr Congreve had known from his childhood.

The garden is spectacular in spring, when many of the 2,000 rhododendron and azalea varieties are in flower, though the most glorious display is offered by the magnolias (300 varieties). The massing of thousands of spring bulbs adds greatly to the scene, as does the extensive planting of clematis on tripods and up trees. Few gardens can boast as many conifers (630 varieties) and none the range of acers (317 varieties). The collections of camellias, berberis, prunus, viburnums, pieris, cornus, and ericas, among others, are all remarkably complete and continue to be enlarged annually as new cultivars become available.

Further variation in the garden is achieved through dramatic architectural incidents. An old quarry has been made into an alpine garden with a Chinese pagoda; there is a terrace with a round moon gate, as well as rock fissures with streams and pools. In addition to all of this, the garden contains a wonderful old walled garden with lawns and herbaceous borders, presided over by a large Georgian glasshouse. Beyond lies another garden, with an extensive collection of herbaceous plants, arranged in order of monthly flowering, and a pond surrounded by 100 forms of Japanese iris.

Bluebells flourishing in the dappled light against a backdrop of azaleas and rhododendrons.

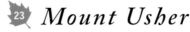

23 *Mount Usher*

Location: On main Dublin–Wexford road outside Ashford

open: Early Mar to Oct, daily, 10.30am–6pm

Further information from:
Philomena O'Dowd, Mount Usher Gardens, Ashford, Co Wicklow
Tel: 0404 40205
Fax: 0404 40205
e-mail: mount.ushergardens@indigo.ie
Website: www.wicklow.ie

Nearby sights of interest:
Arklow Maritime Museum: summer, Mon to Sat, 9am–5pm; Tel: 0402 32868; Avoca Handweavers: all year, daily, 9.30am–6pm; Tel: 0402 35105.

This is a beautifully designed and authentically Robinsonian garden which never fails to enchant. Much of its character is determined by the River Vartry, which flows through it, providing a sense of space and fluidity, while masterfully designed vistas on each side enable more than 4,000 plant varieties, mostly trees and shrubs, to be displayed without any perception of crowding in this 9ha (22 acre) garden. The views upriver and downriver are magical, especially from the garden's four bridges, while the sound of water tumbling over the weirs adds to the delights.

The garden is entered through a courtyard, and a winding path leads visitors past a pavilion dedicated to three generations of the Walpole family, who developed the garden from 1868 until its sale to Mrs Jay in 1980. Down the slope a maple walk leads the eye to the river, with its rich and varied planting, while south of the suspension bridge lies the main woodland garden, with a wealth of shrubs. The croquet lawn is memorable for a magnificent *Tsuga canadensis* 'Pendula', while the azalea ride, a blaze of yellow, red, and white in spring, has an august *Pinus montezumae*, planted in 1905. A grove of spectacular eucalyptus nearby has over 70 varieties, while across the bridge a broad, grassy area lined with Chusan palms extends outwards from the house. In this part of the garden visitors will find excellent collections of nothofagus and eucryphia, the latter with clumps of the hybrid *Eucryphia* x *nymansensis* 'Mount Usher'. Near the house, amid spreading lawns, a mill race plays host to ferns, while the many little paths of the "island" overflow with herbaceous perennials, framed by colourful trees and shrubs, such as a glorious *Magnolia* x *veitchii*.

Banks of hostas and primulas in the stream garden beneath acers and flowering cherries.

Facing page: The River Vartry gives the garden a feeling of openness and splendid vistas.

Powerscourt

Location: On outskirts of Enniskerry; well signposted

open: Mar to Oct, daily, 9.30am–5.30pm; Nov to Feb, daily, 9.30am to dusk; closes 25–6 Dec

Further information from:
Sarah Slazenger, Powerscourt, Enniskerry, Co Wicklow
Tel: 01 204 6000
Fax: 01 286 3561
e-mail: gardens@powerscourt.ie
Website: www.powerscourt.ie

Nearby sights of interest:
Powerscourt Waterfall; Enniskerry.

Few gardens have a more spectacular setting than Powerscourt, and fewer still have a design which so successfully blends house, formal garden, and natural landscape in such a seamless and pleasing way. The breathtaking amphitheatre of descending terraces, the monumental stairway, antique statuary, and the Triton Pool, combined with a wooded park and mountains beyond, seem like a work of inspired genius, though in fact the whole is the product of 250 years of constant evolution. The areas accessible to the public cover about 18ha (45 acres) and, apart from the central axis, there is a circuit path which takes visitors to all the main incidents: the Pepperpot Tower, the Japanese garden, the walled gardens, and the fine tree collections. Visitor numbers can be very high, especially now that the house incorporates a

The 18th-century Perspective Gates once formed part of the screen in Bamberg Cathedral, Bavaria.

The long Herbaceous Border, looking down towards the English Gate.

The central perron, made of local granite and pebbles, looking down on the parterres and terraces.

The Pepperpot Tower was built for the Prince of Wales's visit to Powerscourt in 1911.

The Japanese Garden was made by the eighth viscount on reclaimed bogland in 1908.

Victory, one of a pair with Fame amid alternating stone figures and urns on the upper terrace.

The Vine Gates, leading into the herbaceous border, were wrought in Venice during the 1890s for the seventh Viscount Powerscourt.

"shopping experience", and the best time fully to appreciate the gardens is a weekday morning.

The focus of the garden is a Palladian mansion built in the 1730s and recently rebuilt to accommodate shops and offices after a disastrous fire in 1974. The architect Richard Castle, who designed the house for Richard Wingfield, later the first Viscount Powerscourt, was also responsible for creating the grass terraces and circular pool on the slopes below. These were redesigned a century later by the architect Daniel Robertson, but only the top stone terrace was completed before his patron, the sixth viscount, died in 1844.

The seventh Viscount resumed his father's work when he came of age in 1858, creating the sunken parterres on the middle terrace, the noble staircase flights, and the bronze-painted pegasi by the pool, commissioned from Hagen in Berlin in 1869. The 30m (100ft) high Triton Fountain, based on Bernini's fountain in the Piazza Barberini in Rome, was cast by Kirk in Dublin, while the central perron, the focus of the whole garden, was added in 1875 to a design by Sir Francis Penrose. This imposing Italianate platform, with flanking stairways and cobblestone pavements, incorporates features brought back from the Continent by the seventh viscount, including the 17th-century bronze figures of Æolas from the Palais-Royale in Paris. Many of the fine wrought-iron gates were also added at this time, notably the Chorus Gates and the wonderful Perspective Gates of c1770 from Bamberg Cathedral in Bavaria, both in the walled garden.

The seventh viscount was one of the greatest tree collectors of his age and Powerscourt is filled with many outstanding specimens. These are best viewed by purchasing a copy of the late Alan Mitchell's tree trail at the entrance. Many fine trees are found in the tower valley, notably tall examples of *Pinus coulteri* and *Pseudotsuga japonica* and a very good *Abies nordmanniana*. The focus of this area, the Pepperpot Tower, was built by the eighth viscount in 1911 and modelled on a silver pepperpot in the dining room. Below the valley in a dell is the Japanese Garden, created in 1908, a pleasant area with Chusan palms towering over lawns, ponds, and flowering trees and shrubs. From here a path by the Triton Pool passes a remarkable specimen of Monterey cypress and goes on past a large pet cemetery to the Dolphin Pond, where there are some more fine trees, framed by a line of Japanese cedars. The adjacent walled garden has a very long double herbaceous border and in the top garden there are working glasshouses and colourful displays of hybrid tea roses.

The famous Powerscourt Waterfall lies 3km (2 miles) south of the gardens, within the wildly romantic landscape of the demesne's deer park. With a height of 121m (398ft), it is the highest waterfall in Ireland and is also well worth a visit.

The Triton Fountain and pond, in front of the terraces and steps to the recently rebuilt house.

h open: Apr to Sep, Sun, 2–5pm; other times by appointment

Further information from:
Helen and Bryan Miller,
Shortalstown, Killinick, Co Wexford
Tel: 053 58836

Nearby sights of interest:
Johnstown Castle.

A raised alpine bed encloses a tall eucalyptus tree, with herbaceous borders behind.

Location: Take second right turn off Kilmore road (R739); on right after 2km (1¼ miles)

Shortalstown is an unusually pretty garden, full of decorative inventiveness and richly planted with many rare and tender plants, which thrive in the area's mild climate. From the entrance gates the impressive gravel drive sweeps past mature trees and beautifully maintained herbaceous borders to a pretty 1830s house, incorporating elements of a much earlier residence. The Millers, descendants of the Sealy family, have lived here since the 1600s, while their mature 1ha (2½ acre) garden is the work of three generations of the family from the 1920s.

The area around the house, dominated by a lawn with a Chusan palm, boasts a rockery and tender plants such as *Abutilon vitifolium* and *Crinum longifolium*. A secret garden to one side, screened by a beech hedge, proffers a colourful display of perennials backed with echiums, myrtles, *Eriobotrya japonica*, and other tender shrubs. In front of the house a griselinia hedge, flanked by colourful mixed borders, conceals a vegetable garden that lies along one side of a grass tennis court. Opposite, swirling herbaceous borders are filled with alliums, lobelias, campanulas, phlox, macleayas, and other perennials, while a shady, damp area by the gate has ferns, phormiums, hostas, and candelabra primulas.

The Bay

Location: On main Gorey–Enniscorthy road (N11), 800m (½ mile) S of Camolin, opposite turn to Carnew

Despite its curious name there is nothing remotely coastal about this delightful country garden. Hidden behind mature trees and neatly clipped hedges, the 0.8ha (2 acre) garden has been developed since 1989 on land adjoining a 19th-century farmhouse. The main area has extensive lawns flowing around serpentine beds of shrubs and perennials. There are a sunken rose garden, a hot border, a pond garden and an area filled with white-flowering summer plants, including feverfew, bergenias, and *Romneya coulteri*. An original idea is a funereal border, containing black violas, hollyhocks, geraniums, and other sombre plants.

open: May to Sep, Sun, 3–6pm; Jul and Aug, Fri, 3–6pm; other times by appointment; children free with adults; no dogs

Further information from:
Frances and Iain McDonald,
The Bay, Camolin, Enniscorthy,
Co Wexford
Tel: 054 83349
Fax: 054 83576

Nearby sights of interest:
Ruins of medieval castle at Ferns.

Valclusa

Location: From Enniskerry, follow signs for Powerscourt Waterfall and pass between cream-coloured gate posts on left at bottom of hill before entrance to waterfall

There is a jungle-like profusion about this garden, which has much to offer lovers of plants and wildlife. The site, overlooking Powerscourt Waterfall, covers 2ha (4½ acres), the lower part dominated by ornamental trees associated with a gentleman's lodge, probably built c1830. The older trees, including a redwood planted in 1856, provide the bones of the present garden, created from the 1960s by Eithne MacSweeny and the current owner, Duncan Forsythe. The style is essentially Robinsonian, encouraging honeysuckles, roses, clematis, and other climbers to grow into the trees and planting a profusion of flowering shrubs beneath the canopy. These include rhododendrons, magnolias, camellias, embothriums, white-flowering escallonias, old roses, and a good collection of hydrangeas.

In the upper, more exposed part of the garden there is a collection of more than 400 herbaceous perennials. Many lie in borders flanking the old drive to the stable yard; they include no fewer than 30 varieties of hosta and 120 varieties of geranium. Here too are watsonias, lobelias, *Acanthus spinosus* 'Lady Moore', and masses of buddleias to attract the butterflies.

open: Apr to Oct, Sat, Sun and Bank Holiday Monday, plus Wed and Fri in May and Jun, 11am–8pm; other times by appointment; not suitable for wheelchairs

Further information from:
Susan and Duncan Forsythe,
Valclusa, Waterfall Road,
Enniskerry, Co Wicklow
Tel: 01 286 9485

Nearby sights of interest:
Powerscourt house, gardens, and waterfall (see pp.104–7)

The herbaceous borders, looking towards the yards.

open: All year, daily

Further information from:
Kilkenny County Council, Kilkenny,
Co Kilkenny
Tel: 056 52699

Nearby sights of interest:
Ruins of Inistioge Priory.

Woodstock

Location: Up hill 1.5km (1 mile) above Inistioge

The 20ha (50 acre) ornamental grounds at Woodstock used to be one of the great gardens of the British Isles. From the 1850s thousands of tourists flocked yearly to admire its remarkable parterres, glasshouses, and unrivalled tree collection. Tragedy struck in 1923 when the house was burnt down, its gardens were abandoned and the magical parkland above the River Nore was filled with commercial conifers. But the garden's ghost never ceased to excite wonderment and in 1998 Kilkenny County Council embarked on an ambitious restoration programme.

The focal point is the shell of the 1747 house, which overlooks the sunken parterre panels of the Winter Garden, built in 1860. The ground falls away to a croquet ground on one side, while a path leads uphill through the arboretum to a walled garden. Beyond lies the partly restored flower-garden terrace created by Lady Louisa Tighe in the 1850s and once aligned on a domed conservatory by Richard Turner. The garden has a rockery, a grotto, and an ornamental dairy, but more memorable features are the silver-fir avenue, planted in 1870, and the Monkey Puzzle Walk.

The Monkey Puzzle Walk was planted in 1845 from stock derived from Archibald Menzies' 1795 expedition to Chile.

Woodville 29

Location: 3km (2 miles) from New Ross on Enniscorthy road (N30), opposite turn-off to Kilkenny over River Barrow

The handsome parkland of this early 19th-century mansion contains a striking water and woodland garden, but the main attraction is an old walled garden, whose magnificent *potager* layout of fruit, vegetables, and flowers is a rare survival from that century. Gravel paths edged by low box and incorporating topiary divide the 0.2ha (½ acre) enclosure into sections, while trained old fruit trees on Victorian espalier frames screen vegetables in the central areas. Colourful borders line the walls, including a blue one with delphiniums, sollyas, echiums, and *Sophora viciifolia*. An adjacent border contains a good mix of dahlias, azaras, and romneyas, while tree peonies and *Myosotidium hortensia* do well on the north-facing wall, together with a good specimen of the red-flowering *Chaenomeles* x *superba* 'Rowallane'. The garden also has an area for alpines, an old rose border, the colourful Friends' Garden, and two adjacent old glasshouses, one filled with peaches and nectarines and the other with grapes, plumbagos, ferns, pot plants, and wonderful red, orange, and yellow abutilons.

open: Apr to Sep, 11am–5pm, by appointment

Further information from:
Peter and Irene Roche, Woodville, New Ross, Co Wexford
Tel: 051 421268

Nearby sights of interest:
Dunbrody Abbey and Visitors' Centre, Campile: Apr to Jun, daily, 10am–6pm; Jul to Aug, daily, 10am–7pm; Tel: 051 88603.

The walled garden's borders, vibrant with summer colour.

111

Key to gardens

1 Amergen
2 Annesgrove
3 Ballynacourty
4 Bantry House
5 Boyce's Garden
6 Bunratty
7 Creagh
8 Derreen
9 Dunloe Castle
   Gardens
10 Fota
11 Glanleam
12 Glengarriff:
   Bamboo Park
13 Glin Castle
14 Hillside
15 Ilnacullin:
   Garnish Island
16 Kinoith: Ballymaloe
   Cookery School
17 Lakemount
18 Lisselan
19 Muckross
20 Vandeleur
   Walled Garden

Ennistymon

N85

Ennis

N67

N68

Kilkee

Kilrush 20

6

3

Mouth of
the Shannon

13

5

Adare

N69

Newcastle West

N21

Charlevil

Tralee

N86

Castleisland

N23

Dingle

N72

Mallo

Dingle Bay

Killorgin

Killarney

L. Leane

9

19

11 Cahirciveen

N70

Kenmare

Macroom

N22

1

8

Glengarriff 12

15

Bandon

K

Bantry Bay

4

N71

18

Dunmanus Bay

Skibbereen

7

Baltimore

Key

═══ Motorways

═══ Principal trunk highways

(3) Gardens

● Major towns and cities

• Towns

South–western Ireland

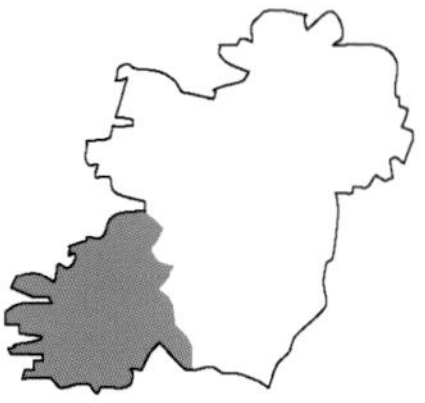

The map labels on the left side:

L. Derg

ERICK

N24

Mitchelstown

Fermoy

N8

Midleton   Youghal

N25

14
10

K

16

The south-western region of Ireland, made up of counties Cork, Kerry, Limerick, and Clare, contains some of the loveliest and most dramatic scenery in all Ireland. Deep, fiord-like inlets punctuate the coastline, facing the Atlantic Ocean and surrounded by the towering mountains of Macgillycuddy's Reeks. Among the many inlets and harbours to the east are the land-locked waters of Cork Harbour, while to the north lie the fertile plains of Limerick's Golden Vale and the long estuary of the River Shannon. In County Clare lies the famous exposed limestone plateau of the Burren, one of the greatest primeval rock gardens in the world.

Grasslands extending high into the mountains bear testament to the amount of rain which this region receives from the moisture-saturated Atlantic winds. With annual falls of around 500cm (200in)

Looking towards the Caha Mountains from the front lawn at Derreen, County Kerry.

a year, the area's gardens are astonishingly lush and luxuriant, but it is the exceptionally mild temperatures which have allowed them to develop their distinctive subtropical character. Frosts are rare in this region of Ireland, with temperatures falling to -2°C (28.5°F) perhaps only four or five times in a bad year, while the January mean for much of the region is 7°C (44.5°F) and that for July is 16°C (70°F).

The most famous of the region's gardens lie amid the grandeur of Kerry's three peninsulas, which point boldly into the ocean. Among these, Ilnacullin on Garnish Island (see pp.130–3), and Derreen (see p.124) illustrate both a typically magical quality and a fascinating range of subtropical plants, especially from Australasia. There are groves of self-seeding tree ferns, enormous cordyline palms, eucalyptuses, and podocarpuses, and rampant forests of tender camellias, rhododendrons, and magnolias, with thick drifts of Asiatic primulas. An equally splendid range of exotics can also be found inland at Annesgrove (see pp.117–18) and Dunloe Castle Gardens (see p.125).

Smaller gardens of the region, which inevitably lay greater emphasis on perennials than on shrubs, make equally good use of the climate. The most outstanding is the wonderfully vibrant garden at Lakemount (see p.135), where skilled mixed planting has created dynamic and challenging contrasts of form, texture, and colour. This garden has inspired many other good gardens in the region, including Amergen (see p.116), Hillside (see p.129), and Boyce's Garden (see p.121), all of which incorporate a distinctive style of interlinking garden compartments. Their clarity and apparent purity of colour, characteristic of all gardens in this region, can be attributed to the clear and bright quality of the light, for the air here is as pure as anywhere in the world.

Clipped bays tower over a colourful scene in the vegetable garden at Kinoith, County Cork.

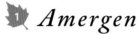

Amergen

open: Apr to Sep, by appointment

Further information from:
Christine Fehily, Amergen, Walshestown, Ovens, Co Cork
Tel: 021 332326

Nearby sights of interest:
ruins of Kilcrea Franciscan Friary; Ballincollig Gunpowder Mill, Ballincollig: Apr to Sep, 10am–6pm; Tel: 021 874430; Blarney Castle: Jun to Aug, 9am–7pm (Sun, 9am–5.30pm); May and Sep, 9am–6.30pm; Oct to Apr, 9am to sunset (Sun, 9.30am to sunset); Tel: 021 385252.

Location: 8km (5 miles) W of Ballincollig on N22; turn right uphill opposite Kelly's pub, take second turn on right and follow cul-de-sac for 1.5km (1 mile)

It usually takes some time to establish a good garden from scratch, but this verdant creation began life only in 1984 and already looks as if it has always been here. The site covers 0.8ha (2 acres) of a hillside around a modern house with lovely views over Inniscarra Reservoir. Belts of birch, evergreen oak, and Monterey cypress provide shelter and the area has been landscaped into separate levels, each with its own character. At the top a long, serpentine lawn flows around beds of shrubs and herbaceous plants. Good spring colour is provided by plants such as *Magnolia dawsoniana* and *M. wilsonii*, while striking effects are gained from *Carpinus orientalis*, *Robinia pseudoacacia* 'Tortuosa', and the unusual *Sambucus nigra* 'Guincho Purple'. There is a collection of grasses around a small pond and nearby are a fine *Azara microphylla*, a *Myrtus* 'Glanleam Gold', and a number of eucalyptuses planted here from seed. A Himalayan fir with amazing violet-purple cones lies below the house and there is also a lovely pink *Buddleia colvilei* here, amid a mixture of dogwoods, lomatias, correas, and tree ferns. Further down the slopes, *Styrax japonicus* makes a great show in June.

On the back terraces, dieramas, penstemons, and other colourful perennials are combined with handsome exotics.

Annesgrove

Location: 16km (10 miles) NW of Fermoy and 3km (2 miles) N of Castletownroche

open: Mid-Mar to end Sep, Mon to Sat, 10am–5pm, Sun, 1–6pm and by appointment

Further information from:
Patrick and Jane Annesley,
Annesgrove, Castletownroche,
Co Cork
Tel: 022 26145
Fax: 022 26145
For the walled garden and
associated nursery contact
Rosamund Henley
Tel: 022 26811 or +086 8291467

Nearby sights of interest:
well-preserved and idyllically
located abbey ruins at Bridgetown
Abbey, Castletownroche.

This charming early 18th-century house, set on the edge of a limestone gorge, is the focus of a wonderfully atmospheric 14ha (35 acre) Robinsonian pleasaunce incorporating a walled garden, a woodland garden, and a river garden. Although there are many surviving Georgian and Victorian features, the gardens are very much the creation of Richard Grove Annesley, a passionate plantsman, who inherited the property in 1907. He subscribed to plant-collecting expeditions, notably of Kingdon Ward, and filled Annesgrove with many rare and tender plants, so that by his death in 1966 it was one of the great gardens of Ireland. His grandson has maintained the gardens since 1973, successfully keeping the wilderness at bay, though visitors should be warned that some of the footpaths and bridges may be considered a hazard.

Garden visitors pass the front of the house, which is cloaked in the evergreen *Euonymus fortunei* and vigorous white-flowering *Actinidia chinensis*. The 18th-century walled garden, typically hidden from the house, was remodelled and compartmentalized in 1907–10, although a Victorian summerhouse on a mound was retained as the central feature. A pretty gate in a wall covered with *Vitis coignetiae* gives access to the area, opening onto a limestone pavement that divides a double herbaceous border backed by yew hedges. At right angles are box-edged ribbon beds filled with annuals, notably mixed petunias, while nearby are borders of Michaelmas daisies, rose beds, and a rustic pergola covered with clematis, roses, and vines. A secluded corner contains a water garden, where a serpentine pool offers a wealth of aquatic and marginal plants beneath a weeping silver birch.

The woodland garden occupies a plateau overlooking the valley and is traversed by the route of a disused avenue. It is best known for its rhododendrons, which in fact occupy only a very confined area, a vein of acid soil discovered by Richard Grove Annesley in the 1920s. Most of the rhododendrons are species rather than hybrids, and many come from seeds introduced

A vibrant mixture of rodgersias, hostas, bergenias, primulas, and irises fringes the pond.

from China by Kingdon Ward. Both the *R. cinnabarinum* and the *R. griersonianum* group are well represented and there are good specimens of *R. falconeri* and *R. delavayi*, among many others.

Magnolias flourish here, such as *M.* x *watsonii*, while the area closer to the house has many fine pieris, dogwoods, and eucryphias and an abundance of hoherias. There are also an vast *Podocarpus salignus* with willow-like foliage; a striking *Aesculus indica* with panicles of pink-flushed flowers in summer; a good *Cercidiphyllum japonicum*, notable for its smoky-pink autumnal colouring; and an excellent drooping *Juniperus recurva* 'Castlewellan'.

A series of narrow, mossy steps, some a little dangerous, leads down to the limestone gorge, where Richard Grove Annesley created his fabulous Giverny-like water garden. He diverted the River Awbeg so that it flowed closer to the house, made weirs, rapids, and an island and built a series of rustic bridges criss-crossing the river. His riverside walks are bordered by groves of bamboo, huge clumps of *Gunnera manicata*, and naturalized colonies of lysichiton, peltiphyllum, polygonums, rodgersias, astilbes, and rare waterlilies. The candelabra primulas are particularly memorable in spring, notably *Primula japonica* and *P. florindae*, the latter being, like so much at Annesgrove, an introduction by Kingdon Ward.

A rustic bridge with glistening lysichitons and cherry blossom at the water's edge.

Ballynacourty

Location: 24km (15 miles) from Limerick, outside Ballysteen, off Limerick–Fownes road

This unusual garden has been expanding since George and Michelina Stackpool acquired the property in 1968. Focused on an attractive well-appointed house, which they built from the ruins of an old cottage, the garden comprises a series of interlinked compartments, embracing some 3.5ha (9 acres) of undulating hillside. The inner garden spreads out from the house as a generous apron of lawn fringed with trees sheltering mixed borders. In one direction paths lead to a small pond enclosed by gunneras and other moisture-loving plants, while in another lie two productive gardens, each behind neat hedges and filled with fruit, vegetables, herbs, and flowers for the house. From this relatively enclosed atmosphere one enters the expansive laburnum garden, with its beds of flowering trees and shrubs set in an expansive lawn. As elsewhere in the garden, old rose varieties are prominent here. More colourful mixed borders lie in the newest compartment, which occupies an exposed position on the hillside above the gardens. From here there are wonderful views of the estuary of the River Shannon.

open: By appointment at any time

Further information from:
George Stackpool
Tel: 061 396409
Fax: 061 396733 (call either number weekdays during working hours)

Nearby sights of interest:
Curraghchase Demesne (former home of Aubrey de Vere and now a Forest Park); Lough Gur Stone Age Centre: May to Sep, daily, 9am–6pm; Tel: 061 360788.

Fortissimo mixed summer borders in Ballynacourty's expansive laburnum garden.

Bantry House

open: Mar to Oct, 9am–6pm

open: All year, daily,
9am–6pm; most spring and
summer evenings until 8pm;
closes 25 Dec

Further information from:
Egerton and Brigitte Shelswell-
White, Bantry, Co Cork
Tel: 027 50047
Fax: 027 50795

Nearby sights of interest:
Bantry Armada Centre, East
Stables, Bantry House: Apr to Oct,
daily, 10am–6pm; Tel: 027 51796
or 51996.

Location: 800m (½ mile) from Bantry town, off Cork road

Bantry House was the first country house in the 20th century to open its doors to the public. Countless thousands of visitors subsequently viewed the fine furnishings of this great theatrical mansion and admired its incomparable setting, which, like a Claude Lorrain painting, gazes out across the bay to the Caha Mountains. The Victorian gardens are quite a new attraction – the fruits of a continuing restoration project.

Formally arranged around the mansion, the gardens were created during the periods 1844–8 and 1858–67 by Richard White, who became second Earl of Bantry on his father's death in 1851. Having assumed control of the family estates in 1844, he enlarged the house, transforming it from a modest Georgian residence into a setting for the magnificent treasures he had acquired during his Continental travels. As an amateur artist, evidently fully aware of the prevailing architectural gardening styles, he grasped the potential of the site to devise a sensational axial layout of terracing, balustrades, statuary, and parterres: features then the height of fashion, but rarely used to such dramatic effect.

The north terraces, which visitors normally see first, were created to hide the road that had been constructed along the shore in 1843. Hundreds of labourers, taking up much-needed employment during the Great Famine of 1845–8, moved vast amounts of soil to create descending grass terraces, which incorporate long balustrading, urns, and statues of Flora, Hebe, Venus, and Terpsichore. A circular projection in the front balustrade is decorated with cannon and a copy of a Warwick vase, while the two main terraces contain beautifully restored interconnecting beds, very characteristic of 1850s garden taste. Also typical of this era is the embroidered parterre formed of dwarf box on the west side of the house. This would once have relied on coloured gravels for effect, but has since been adapted as a rosary.

The Italian Garden in spring, with the house in the background.

The real garden triumph at Bantry, the "Stairway to the Sky", lies to the rear of the house, where the steep hillside is formed into dramatically rising terraces linked with staircases on an axis with the house. Restored, and decorated with large terracotta pots, these terraces overlook a colourful floral parterre, now meticulously recreated, with a central pond and a circular iron frame that supports wisteria. An immense conservatory once flanked the house's library but has long vanished, as also have iron arcades on both sides of the parterre.

Boyce's Garden

Location: Mountrenchard, 42km (26 miles) from Limerick on N69 to Tralee and 16km (10 miles) from Tarbert; signposted at Loughill

Phil and Dick Boyce began this garden in 1982 around their modern house, which has commanding views of the Shannon estuary. Within less than 0.4ha (1 acre) they have created a surprisingly diverse range of intimate garden rooms, all skilfully designed and interlinked in a style inspired by the Cross garden at Lakemount (see p.135). Many colourful and tender plants are used in its many microclimates, not least in the main rockery, which is filled with choice alpines. Nearby is a small lily pond with a miniature fountain, overlooked by a Mediterranean-style summerhouse, while containers filled with cacti of various kinds add to the balmy feel in this corner. A stretch of lawn below the house is flanked by raised beds filled with vibrant herbaceous perennials, such as blue irises, delphiniums, and phloxes, while at the far end a pergola is festooned with roses and clematis. In a small enclosure are a variety of tree peonies with a *Melianthus major*, clumps of lilies, and a spectacular *Rosa* 'Nevada', while tree ferns, a golden *Sophora tetraptera*, and other tender plants add an exotic touch. Nearby lie a fern bed, a vegetable garden, and a small glasshouse with a vine. On the opposite side of the house, strips of lawn are flanked by a mixture of trees and shrubs, including a spiral topiary, phormiums, golden bamboo, hibiscus, rhododendrons, and camellias.

open: May to Oct, daily, 10am–6pm; all year by appointment

Further information from:
Mr and Mrs Boyce
Tel: 069 65302

Nearby sights of interest:
Desmond Hall and Great Hall at Newcastlewest; ruins of medieval convent at Shanagolden.

Parts of this small garden have a strong Mediterranean feel.

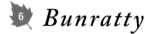

Bunratty

Location: On Limerick–Ennis road, in Folk Park

open: Sep to May, daily, 9.30am–5.30pm (last admission to Folk Park 4.30pm); Jun to Aug, 9am–6.30pm (last admission to Folk Park 5.30pm); closes Good Friday and 24–6 Dec

Further information from:
Head Office, Bunratty Castle and Folk Park, Co Clare
Tel: 061 360788
Fax: 061 361020
Freefone: 1800 269811

An old walled garden of 0.2ha (½ acre) near Bunratty House, built in 1804, is the setting for an ornamental flower garden laid out in the Regency manner. It was designed by Belinda Jupp as an attraction for visitors to the Folk Park and contains plants known from the early 19th century. The main area, which is dissected by crossing paths, has an arbour clad in *Clematis orientalis* and geometric beds centred on *Phillyrea angustifolia*. At one end are pots with agapanthus, while at the other rose hoops support damask roses, *R.* 'Ispahan' and 'Madame Hardy' in circular thyme beds. Outside the enclosure a Regency shrubbery has been made, while in the Folk Park a number of vernacular buildings are complemented by sympathetic gardens.

Creagh

Location: 6km (3¾ miles) S of Skibbereen on Baltimore road (D595)

open: Mar to Oct, daily except Tue, 10am–6pm and by appointment

Further information from:
Martin Sherry, Gwendoline and Peter Harold-Barry Trust, Skibbereen, Co Cork
Tel: 028 22121
Fax: 028 22121

Nearby sights of interest:
Fishing port of Baltimore, where boats sail for Clear Island and Sherkin Island (keyholder for friary ruins on Sherkin Island: Mary O'Neill); Drombeg Stone Circle.

The Balubah summerhouse echoes the curve of the main house.

This enchanting garden is set in the wooded grounds of an old demesne that extends down to the sea estuary of the River Ilex. Acquired by the late Peter and Gwendoline Harold-Barry in 1945, the property was developed into an informal Robinsonian garden covering 8ha (20 acres). Utilizing existing features, they created a network of paths across glades, through woodlands and along the shore, enabling visitors to admire a wide range of tender plants in this mild and moist part of Ireland.

A seductive, ochre-painted Regency house, built for William Wrixton-Beecher as a summer residence, forms the focal point of the garden. It looks out on sweeping lawns fringed with trees and shrubs, including many hydrangeas, which make a great show in late summer, as does a collection of over 30 tender fuchsias on a terrace wall. Nearby a *Datura sanguinea* with trumpets flowers in May, like many other tender plants here. These include white-flowering *Leptospermum scoparium*, many handsome varieties of abutilon, mimosa, and tree peony, and superb specimens of the fiery *Embothrium coccineum*, all of which, like numerous camellias, rhododendrons, azaleas, and magnolias, have been planted along woodland paths and glades.

In a dell near the house stands a thatched summerhouse, inspired by Congolese Balubah tribal huts, close to which is a crimson-flowering monga waratah (*Telopea mongaensis*) from New South Wales. Paths leading to the serpentine pond pass a variety of notable plants: a *Magnolia campbellii*, a large *Myrtus communis*, the vanilla-scented *Azara microphylla* 'Variegata', and the single-flowering *Camellia japonica* 'Jupiter'. The planting along the edge of the serpentine pond was inspired by the work of Henri Rousseau ("Le Douanier"), the Parisian artist who painted the tropical jungle but never left his own city. In the cool shade grow a profusion of green foliage plants: gunneras, lysichitons, phormiums, Chusan palms, weeping willows, blechnum ferns, *Dicksonia antarctica*, and *Aralia japonica*, and flashes of seasonal colour are provided by arum lilies, hydrangeas, and irises. There is a *Viburnum cylindricum* at the far end, near which one may see the Gothick windows of a ruined gazebo peering out through the undergrowth.

The walled garden is approached through groves of pittosporum, camellias, and rhododendrons, including *R. macabeanum* and the crimson-flowering 'Tally Ho' by the gate. There are orderly rows of vegetables inside, some new glasshouses and exotic varieties of fowl. Nearby is a long, mixed border, while other attractions include the Jungle Walk and Sir John's Walk, the latter bringing one through Monterey pines to the shore.

Colourful gardens surround the house in springtime.

open: Apr to Sep, daily,
11am–6pm; best in Apr and May

Further information from:
The Hon David Bigham, Lauragh,
Co Kerry
Tel: 064 83103 (or Jacky Ward,
the gardener)

Nearby sights of interest:
Magnificent scenic views from
Healy Pass above Lauragh;
Kenmare; Kenmare Heritage
Centre: Easter to end Sep, daily,
10am–6pm; Tel: 064 41233 or
31633.

Tree ferns and rhododendrons
beneath the woodland canopy.

Derreen

Location: 24km (15 miles) SW of Kenmare and just N of Lauragh

Most gardens fade from memory, but the sights and scents of Derreen in spring are an experience unlikely to be forgotten in a lifetime of garden visits. Occupying the whole of a 36ha (90 acre) peninsula in a sheltered inlet amid the shimmering waters of Kilmackilloge Bay and the wild, majestic Caha Mountains, this is a subtropical Elysium of luxuriant vegetation enjoying the benign microclimate of the Kerry coastline. Forests of naturalized tree ferns, groves of bamboo, towering eucalyptus, stupendous rhododendrons, and a range of exotic trees and shrubs clamber over moss-covered boulders and chasms in this exhilarating and most skilfully designed Robinsonian garden.

Derreen is the creation of the fifth Marquess of Lansdowne, who for 60 years from 1870 transformed the rocky peninsula, planting it with pines, oaks, *Olearia albida*, *Pittosporum tenuifolium*, and griselinias to establish his garden. It was designed around a modest mid-19th-century house, the surrounding lawns of which sweep down to the woodland below. In these woods visitors will find a profusion of azaleas, rhododendrons, drimys, myrtles, leptospermums, kalmias and pernettyas crowding a labyrinth of mossy paths.

The best time to appreciate the gardens is spring, when the rhododendrons are in flower. These include a magnificent *Rhododendron falconeri*, a large *R. sinogrande*, and clumps of 'Loderi King George', *R. keysii*, *R. griffithianum*, and *R. niveum*. Among other notable plants here are a beautiful *Pinus patula*, an attractive *Thujopsis dolabrata*, and a remarkable *Cryptomeria japonica* 'Elegans', lying recumbent over a path. But the chief glory of Derreen is a grove of tree ferns, *Dicksonia antarctica*, along the course of the evocatively named "King's Oozy". These have become naturalized beneath the jade-stemmed bamboos and Tasmanian blue gums.

Dunloe Castle Gardens

Location: 8km (5 miles) W of Killarney and 1.5km (1 mile) S of Beaufort, on road to Gap of Dunloe

open: Apr to Oct, daily; groups by appointment

The magnificent panoramic views of the towering Macgillycuddy's Reeks was the main reason why Howard Harrington, a rich American, decided to settle here and create this splendid garden. Despite its exposed and elevated position, he succeeded in establishing an extensive range of trees and shrubs between 1922 and 1936. Windbreaks were planted for the arboretum, while an old walled garden was used for his choice plants. The garden was subsequently maintained by Agnes Petitt until 1960, when it was acquired by a German-owned hotel group, which decided to expand the collections. Advice was sought from Gerd Krussmann, Roy Lancaster and Harold Hillier, and consequently the range of plants has increased considerably in recent decades.

The main arboretum lies in front of the conference hall attached to the large 1960s hotel. Among the most interesting plants here are a curious hornbeam from Asia, *Carpinus cordata*, and the hybrid hazel *Corylus* x *colurnoides*. There are rare maples and Chinese cherry trees, including *Prunus litigiosa*, discovered by the Irish plant hunter Augustine Henry. Another of his introductions, *Carpinus henryana*, lies at the end of the arboretum, close to a rarely seen conifer from Taiwan, *Calocedrus formosana*.

Amid good collections of maples, rhododendrons and azaleas there are many fine tender plants in the walled garden, such as the South African shrub *Bowkeria gerrardiana*, the Chilean foliage plant *Lomatia ferruginea*, and a *Viburnum odoratissimum* from China. Close to the 13th-century castle stands an *Arbutus unedo*, native to County Kerry, while some distance to the south-west lies the real treasure of Dunloe: a Chinese pond cypress (*Glyptostrobus lineatus*), which, at over 9m (30ft) high, must be one of the largest in cultivation.

Further information from:
Dunloe Castle Hotel, Dunloe,
Co Kerry
Tel: 064 31900 or 44111
Fax: 064 44583

Nearby sights of interest:
Gap of Dunloe; Kerry Bog Museum (Glenbeigh): Mar to Nov, daily, 8.30am–7pm; Tel: 066 69184.

Banks of azaleas catch the light beneath the tree canopy.

125

open: 17 Mar to 3 Nov, weekdays, 10am–6pm, Sun, 11am–6pm

Further information from:
Dúchas – The Heritage Service
Tel: 021 812678

Nearby sights of interest:
Barryscourt Castle and Tudor gardens, Carrigtohill: daily, 10am–5pm; Tel: 021 883864; in Cobh, or Queenstown, an attractive old naval town, the story of emigration can be explored in the Queenstown Centre: daily, 10am–6pm; Tel: 021 813591.

The Pond Garden, with its lush plantings, is set in the middle of the Arboretum.

 # *Fota*

Location: 14.5km (9 miles) east of Cork city on Cobh (Queenstown) road; signposted

The famous collection of trees and shrubs at Fota incorporates many historically important specimens that are numbered among the earliest introductions of their kind. The plantings began in the 1820s when the Smith-Barrys built their splendid Regency mansion here and began to lay out ornamental grounds. These developed to cover 12ha (30 acres) and now embrace an arboretum, a small lake, and a rock garden for ferns and walled gardens. A magnificent landscaped park, now partly despoiled by a golf course, surrounds the house and gardens and occupies the whole of the 316ha (780 acre) island of Fota (or Foaty), whose sheltered location in this tidal estuary contributes to the mild microclimate enjoyed by the gardens.

The oldest areas are focused on the majestic lawns adjacent to the house. From here wrought-iron gates lead into the walled Italian Garden, where a magnificent specimen of *Magnolia grandiflora* 'Goliath' shades a charming little temple. Sadly, most of the original plantings here have gone, but one survival is a rather showy *Colquhounia coccinea* var. *mollis*. The walls are lined with colourful herbaceous borders, while an adjacent enclosure is devoted to roses. A handsome camphor tree, *Cinnamomum*

camphora, features in the border outside, and there is also a fuchsia collection here. Nearby stands a recently restored mid-19th-century orangery flanked by *Phoenix canariensis*.

Fota is noted for its magnolia collection, its most famous specimen being a 23m (75ft) tall *Magnolia campbellii* planted in 1872. The collection lies on the east side of the grounds, together with a large collection of rhododendrons. Among the plantings here is a fine *Eriobotrya japonica*, but it would be difficult to start noting all the superb trees at Fota, as there are so many. But mention should be made of a *Cryptomeria japonica* 'Spiralis' and a *Dacrydium franklinii*, both planted in the 1850s and the largest of their kinds in Europe. The future of all these fine plantings was in the balance for many years, but the gardens are now being revitalized by Dúchas – the Heritage Service, which assumed control in the late 1990s.

 Glanleam

Location: On E side of Valentia Island about 1.5km (1 mile) from Knightstown; signposted

open: May to Sep, daily, 10am–5pm

This is no longer the great garden it was a century ago, but it retains much of interest amid a wild, jungle-like beauty. It covers about 16ha (40 acres) around the former ancestral home of the Knights of Kerry, and offers commanding views across Dingle Bay. The garden was started c1832 by Sir Peter Fitzgerald, 19th Knight (1808–80), who began by planting windbreaks of escallonia, sycamore, Monterey cypress, and Monterey pine. Above the house he built a 1ha (2½ acre) walled garden, still partly in use, and below laid out a labyrinth of paths flanked by an outstanding collection of southern hemisphere plants. Many collected by William Lobb in Chile in the 1840s are still there: a monkey puzzle, enormous crinodendrons, and the largest embothriums in the British Isles. The tallest examples of *Clethra arborea* (lily of the valley tree) and *Cordyline australis* in these islands are also here. There are tall specimens of pittosporum, a forest of tree ferns, and many cordylines, date palms, and phormiums amid tender exotics such as the South African arum lily (*Zantedeschia aethiopica*) and the blackwood (*Acacia melanoxylon*). *Myrtus apiculata* is naturalized here, and it was a variegated form discovered in this garden in the 1960s that gave rise to the famous 'Glanleam Gold' variety.

Further information from:
Meta and Jessica Kreissig,
Glanleam House, Co Kerry
Tel: 066 9476176
Fax: 066 9476108

Nearby sights of interest:
Magnificent scenery around Valentia Island; Skellig Heritage Centre on the island: Apr to Sep, daily, 10am–6.30pm; Jun to Aug, 9.30am–6pm; Tel: 066 76306.

Date palms, phormiums, and other exotic foliage bristling beneath the canopy.

Glengarriff: Bamboo Park

Location: On N71 from Bantry to Glengarriff; gates on left just before harbour

open: Easter to 31 Oct, daily, 10am–6pm; Jun to Aug, 10am–9pm

Further information from:
Claudine Caluwaerts, Glengarriff
Bamboo Park Ltd, Glengarriff,
Co Cork
Tel: 027 63570
Fax: 027 63255

Nearby sights of interest:
Ilnacullin gardens, Garnish Island
(see pp.130–3).

This garden is an attempt to create a Chinese jungle garden on the shore of Glengarriff Bay. Opened in 2000, it covers about 2ha (5 acres) and incorporates gravel walks, a stone-lined pond, and plantings of more than 30 different varieties of bamboo, from the genera *Arundinaria*, *Sasa*, *Chusquea*, and *Phyllostachys*. In addition many date palms and tree ferns have been planted and, given the mild, moist conditions that prevail locally, should do well. The oriental-style buildings at the entrance are out of place, but the wonderful walk along the shore, which offers views of the bay, makes the garden worth a visit.

Glin Castle

Location: On N69 between Fownes and Tarbert; turn left into Glin village and right at top of square

open: May to Jun, daily, 10am–12 noon and 3–4pm; closes Tue, other times by appointment

open: By appointment

Further information from:
Bob Duff (manager), Glin Castle,
Glin, Co Limerick
Tel: 068 34112 or 34173
Fax: 068 34364
e-mail: knight@iol.ie
Website: www.glincastle.com

The seat of the Knights of Glin, who have lived hereabouts for more than 500 years, dates to the 1780s, while its crenellations and Gothic details were added in the 1820s. It has a timeless air, much enhanced by white walls and a magical setting, nestling in trees, overlooking the River Shannon. The parkland is essentially late 18th-century with Regency alterations, and the gardens retain elements of two centuries of continuous evolution.

The primary area of ornamental planting lies south of the house, where the main lawn is divided by an axial path aligned on a beautiful *Parrotia persica*. This was planted in the 1930s by Veronica Villiers, the 28th knight's wife, who formalized the area with balls of clipped bay below the house and yew hedges in the lawn centre. She planted magnolias, dogwoods, and cherries on the lawn fringes, where an impressive *Pinus radiata* and other stately trees hold sway. Walks beyond this lead to a stream that runs through a 19th-century pleasure ground, where the paths are flanked by myrtles, camellias, hydrangeas, and rhododendrons. In a glade close to the walled garden visitors will find a charming early 19th-century hermitage, restored in recent years.

A view across the walled garden, with the tidal estuary of the Shannon in the background.

The walled garden at Glin is still a picking garden, full of immaculately tended flowers, fruit, and vegetables destined for use in the house. One of the paths in the walled garden is lined with clipped yews which are aligned on a semicircular bench, while another path is aligned on a rustic temple which protects a headless statue of Andromeda chained to her rock. The grey stone walls of this garden support fig trees, pears, and clematis, and amid the lines of vegetables and cut flowers there stands a Gothic henhouse.

 # *Hillside*

Location: Glounthane road (off Waterford road); go up hill at church, pass under bridge, then through entrance marked "Annmount", and take first turn on left

This charming informal garden of 1.5ha (4 acres), begun in 1979, occupies a hillside clearing in the old demesne woods of Annmount. It enjoys a mild microclimate, and the sloping ground, mostly south-facing, is divided into interlinked garden areas, each making best use of the changing levels.

Adjacent to the modern house is a terrace and rockery, the latter occupying the steepest slope in the garden. A circular pool at the top, fringed with alstroemeria and other bright perennials, feeds a little stream which cascades down rocks amid ferns to a small pond with hostas, small-leafed gunneras, phormiums, and grasses, notably *Hakonechloa macra* 'Aureola'.

The rockery above has dwarf conifers and alpines, including hardy geraniums, while swirling lawns below are encompassed by mixed borders beneath the trees. Here the exotic foliage of phormiums and cordylines blends with a wide range of shrubs providing seasonal colour, among them rhododendrons and azaleas, dogwoods, acers, and hydrangeas. There are magnolias, such as the late-flowering *Magnolia sieboldii*, and a large tulip tree. More alpines occupy a scree bed, together with bulbs, dwarf rhododendrons, grevilleas, and a collection of celmisias, while above the house a border of pale herbaceous plants is framed by the ascending horizontal branches of *Viburnum plicatum* 'Mariesii'.

open: During Cork's Glorious Gardens Season (7–16 Jun); other times by appointment

Further information from:
Mary Byrne, Annmount, Glounthane, Co Cork
Tel: 021 353119

Nearby sights of interest:
Barryscourt Castle and Tudor gardens, Carrigtohill: daily, 10am–5pm; Tel: 021 883864.

Echiums tower above shrubs and herbaceous perennials.

15
Ilnacullin: Garnish Island

open: Apr to Jun and Sep, Mon to Sat, 10am–4.30pm, Sun, 10am–4.30pm; Jul and Aug, Mon to Sat, 10am–6.30pm, Sun, 1–7pm; Mar and Oct, Mon to Sat, 9.30am–6.30pm, Sun, 11am–7pm

Further information from:
Finbarr O'Sullivan, Dúchas – The Heritage Service, Garnish Island, Glengarriff, Co Cork
Tel: 027 63040
Fax: 027 63187

Nearby sights of interest:
from Glengarriff there are delightful drives around the dramatic coastline of Bantry Bay.

Location: On island in Bantry Bay, 1.5km (1 mile) by boat from Glengarriff

This famous garden island of 15ha (37 acres), set in the diadem of west Cork's splendid coastal scenery, is linked to the mainland by frequent ferries that leave from three separate jetties in the village. Visitors find themselves in a subtropical paradise which few realize was little more than a bare, windswept rock 100 years ago.

Ilnacullin's transformation, surely one of the 20th century's great gardening achievements, began in 1910, when the island, complete with its Martello tower, was purchased from the War Office by a Belfast businessman, John Annan Bryce. He commissioned

The Renaissance-style campanile rises above the walled garden and provides a striking landmark throughout the island.

Peto's splendid wisteria-clad Casita gazes down on the pool of the sunken Italian Garden and its venerable bonsai specimens.

The Martello tower was erected in 1805 on the highest point of the island to fend off a feared Napoleonic invasion.

The small, roofless Grecian temple, mounted on a viewing terrace, overlooks the sea.

the English architect Harold Peto to design a garden here, and from 1911 to 1914 over 100 men were engaged in the task. They moved huge quantities of soil to the island, blasted rock, laid paths, and built a walled garden, a clock tower, and an Italian Garden. Peto's use of classical architecture, combined with rich sweeps of Robinsonian planting, proved brilliantly successful in this island setting. However, it was not until the great Scottish plantsman Murdo Mackenzie came to look after the garden in 1928 that the island really came into its own. Over a period of 50 years "Mac" developed the garden into one of Ireland's horticultural showpieces.

The centrepiece of Peto's creation is the Italian Garden and its wisteria-covered Casita. This beguiling colonnaded building of Bath stone, which once housed Bryce's collection of Old Master drawings, overlooks a sunken garden featuring a pool, a pavilion, and the distant landscape beyond: a much-vaunted chocolate-box view that will be familiar to many visitors. The varied planting here epitomizes the way in which the climatic advantages of the island have been used to assemble a rich collection of shrubs from the southern hemisphere. There are tender fuchsias, abutilons, myrtles, olearias, and cestrums, a variety of the sun-loving callistemons and unusually large leptospermum shrubs, including the pink-flowering manuka, *Leptospermum scoparium* 'Nicholasii'. Here too are examples of the curious *Corokia cotoneaster* and the tropical South American shrub *Cassia corymbosa*, while a magnificent *Drimys winteri* scents

The clock tower protruding above Garnish Island's verdant vegetation, with the Caha Mountains in the distance.

the air in spring. A plant to note is *Callistemon salignus* 'Murdo Mackenzie', while elsewhere other sports of local significance include a bicolour tea-tree (*Leptospermum scoparium* 'Rowland Bryce'), and the variegated *Griselinia littoralis* 'Bantry Bay', discovered by Mackenzie c1950.

The pool, glimpsed though the colonnades of the Italian Garden's Casita.

Another of Peto's contributions is the long, grassy glade known as Happy Valley. This begins at the Grecian Temple and culminates in the steps that lead up to the Martello tower. Of the many varied trees and shrubs along here most worthy of note are the pendulous *Dacrydium franklinii*, superb specimens of *Agathis australis* and *Lyonothamnus aspleniifolius*, a remarkably tall *Chamaecyparis lawsoniana* 'Ellwoodii', and some good rhododendrons.

The walled garden, dominated by an Italianate clock tower, is in 16 sections and crossed by a long, colourful herbaceous border with attractive matching gates at either end. One of the cross paths focuses on a sarcophagus overhung by a specimen of *Michelia doltsopa*, but sadly most of this large garden is now overrun with equisetum and other weeds. This dereliction reflects a general decline here over the past 20 years, despite the staff's heroic efforts. Successive Irish governments have refused to grant enough staff and resources to maintain this remarkable garden adequately.

The entrance to the walled garden, looking down the herbaceous border.

open: Apr to Oct, daily,
9.30am–6pm

Further information from:
Tim and Darina Allen, Ballymaloe
Cookery School, Shanagarry,
Midleton, Co Cork
Tel: 021 646785 or 646909

Nearby sights of interest:
Jameson Heritage Centre,
Midleton: Mar to Oct, daily,
9am–4.30pm; Tel: 021 613594;
Cloyne Cathedral and Round
Tower; Youghal, for its town walls,
medieval church and abbey ruins.

A willow-skirted scarecrow
stands guard over the vegetables
and flowers in the *potager*.

16 *Kinoith: Ballymaloe Cookery School*

Location: Signposted from Castlemartyr–Ballycotton road

Good cuisine and gardening make natural bedfellows. Rarely is this so effectively demonstrated as at Kinoith, where 3ha (8 acres) of decorative gardens supply a dazzling range of top-quality vegetables, fruit, and herbs for the adjacent cookery school and the renowned Ballymaloe House Hotel.

After the cookery school was established in 1983 the overgrown beech hedges of the abandoned gardens here were restored. One enclosure has an Edwardian flower garden, and another was made into a herb garden inspired by Villandry, with box-edged beds enclosing an array of culinary and medicinal plants, including edible flowers, violas, marigolds, and beds of sea kale beneath terracotta cloches. Beyond this lies a lawn with specimen trees, a pond, a temple, and a remarkable 90m (300ft) long double herbaceous border aligned on a hexagonal gazebo, the interior of which is covered with shells laid in intricate designs by Charlotte Kerr-Wilson. Adjacent to the school is an ornamental fruit garden, while a screen of trees hides a beautiful *potager* filled with seasonal vegetables.

Lakemount

Location: Just N of Glanmire, passing bridge on right and take first turn to left up hill and over the brow; garden lies on left, entered through a pedestrian gate

open: Mar to Oct, every afternoon, by appointment

Lakemount is one of Ireland's most celebrated late 20th-century gardens. Founded in 1953 by Mrs Peggy Cross and developed by her son Brian, a well-known gardener-writer, it occupies 2ha (5½ acres) and has spectacular views over the River Lee. It is noted for its plantsmanship and rich assemblage of plants, all of which have been superbly integrated into their setting.

One of Lakemount's hallmarks is the skilful interlinking of separate areas without compartmentalization. Fronting the house, a lawn flows around borders filled with rhododendrons, azaleas, primulas, and meconopsis intermixed with drifts of sparkling perennials, such as watsonias, lobelias, crocosmias, aconitums, and cautleyas. Daphnes, pieris, and hydrangeas are much in evidence, the last particularly concentrated east of the house. To the south lies a bog garden and nearby is a winter garden, notable for its hellebores, while east of the house a paved courtyard boasts an alpine scree garden. A conservatory in a tiny yard behind the courtyard is filled with tender plants, among them abutilons, daturas, cassias, and veltheimias in pots. There is a kitchen garden and an arboretum of 1.5ha (3½ acres) with a good collection of acers.

Further information from:
Brian Cross, Glanmire, Co Cork
Tel: 021 821052

Nearby sights of interest:
Dunkathel House: May to Oct, Wed to Sun, 2–4pm; Cork Public Museum, Mardyke: Jun to Aug, Mon to Fri, 11am–5pm, Sat, 3–5pm; Tel: 021 270679; Munster Literature Centre (25 Sullivan's Quay): Jun to Dec, Mon, Tue and Thu to Sat, 11am–6pm, Wed, 2–9pm, Sun, 12 noon–5pm.

Skilful positioning of ornaments is a feature of this garden.

Lisselan

18

open: Mar to Oct, daily,
8am–7pm; groups by appointment

Further information from:
John Bevan, Lisselan Estate Office,
Lisselan, Clonakilty, Co Cork
Tel: 023 33249
Fax: 023 34605

Nearby sights of interest:
Lisnagun Rath, Darrara, a restored
10th-century farmstead.

**Candelabra primulas soften the
approach to a rustic bridge.**

Location: Entrance signposted 2.5km (1½ miles) E of Clonakilty on main
Cork–Clonakilty road (N71)

Lisselan was one of a number of ambitious gardening schemes
undertaken in Ireland during the Edwardian era. It lies on the
banks of the River Argideen, beneath a romantic French château-
style house built in the 1850s. Using William Robinson's
published textbooks as a guide, Mrs Reginald Bence-Jones
created the gardens between 1903 and 1910. They included a
rockery, a bog garden, a rose garden, an American Garden, a lake,
and other features, many of which are still present despite severe
damage caused by the building of a golf course in recent years.

A glass conservatory made for the Cork Exhibition of 1902
is still in use, while the high terrace around the
house added in 1903 leads onto the steep rockery,
now planted with shrubs such as cistus and erica.
The gardens below, notable for their spring
colour, particularly azaleas, lead to the water's
edge, where there are a small summerhouse, rustic
bridges, and much colourful waterside planting.
Other features include a fine rhododendron ground
and a 21m (70ft) long, rose-wreathed pergola,
now sadly spoiled by an adjacent golf tee.

Muckross

19

open: All year, daily,
9am–5.30pm; closes for one week
at Christmas
open: Mid-Mar to Jun, Sep
and Oct, 9am–6pm; Jul and Aug,
9am–7pm; Nov to mid-Mar,
9am–5.30pm; closes for one
week at Christmas

Further information from:
The Manager, Dúchas – The
Heritage Service, Muckross House,
Killarney, Co Kerry
Tel: 064 31440

Nearby sights of interest:
Muckross Friary: mid-Jun to early
Sep, daily, 10am–5pm; Tel: 066
13111.

Location: 5km (3 miles) S of Killarney on Kenmare road (N71)

Situated in a magical position beside the Lower Lough at
Killarney, the gardens and house of Muckross lie within a vast
estate given to the nation by Arthur Vincent in 1932. Historically,
the property belonged to the Herberts, who built a great
Elizabethan-style mansion of silvery-grey Portland stone here in
1839–44 to the designs of the Scottish architect William Burn.
From 1899 to 1910 the property belonged to Lord Ardilaun and
was then sold to William Bourne, a rich American, who gave it to
his daughter Maud and her husband Arthur Vincent.

In the years before the outbreak of World War I in 1914,
the Vincents commissioned the garden designer R Wallace to
make a Renaissance-style sunken garden adjacent to the house.
Overlooking this garden, an enormous tiered rockery was
constructed, with winding paths to the top. This was apparently
designed for alpines, but the rainfall at Muckross – 170cm (67in)
annually – is so great that these never flourished. The rockery is

now a shrubbery, and among the plants here are *Euonymus alatus* and *Acer palmatum* var. *heptalobum* 'Ôsakazuki'.

The area between the house and the lake is occupied by expansive lawns, majestic Scots pines and huge clumps of *Rhododendron arboreum*. This inspired piece of landscaping, which is breathtaking against the distant purple mountains, was probably the work of the famous garden designer Edward Milner, who worked here in the mid-19th century. On the perimeter of the lawns is a stream garden with moisture-loving plants and a woodland garden. The latter boasts a large collection of camellia species and hybrids, while other plants include groups of mahonias, cherries, acers and splendid specimens of the white-flowering *Stuartia pseudocamellia* from Japan, *Magnolia* x *soulangeana* 'Brozzonii' and the rare *Atherosperma moschatum* from Australia. The old walled garden has been made into a large ornamental area with restored glasshouses, but gardeners should not leave Muckross without admiring the largest known stand of the indigenous *Arbutus unedo*.

Banks of *Rhododendron arboreum* beneath Scots pine on the lawns.

 # *Vandeleur Walled Garden*

Location: 800m (½ mile) E of Kilrush on Killimer road

The Vandeleur family, originally merchants from Holland, were established in Kilrush in 1687. Eventually they built Kilrush House and became influential during the Regency period, representing County Clare in parliament. Kilrush House was burnt down over a century ago but the beautifully constructed walls of the fruit, flower, and vegetable garden remain intact. As a forgotten garden, Vandeleur Walled Garden has been redesigned for the 21st century around the old path system and specializes in many unusual and tender plants that thrive in the mild local climate. Replanting of the wide borders that line the walls began in spring 2000. The middle of the garden contains the nucleus of a plant collection; other focal points are an unusual water feature and a horizontal maze.

open: Summer, daily, 10am–6pm; winter, Mon to Fri, 10am–4pm

Further information from:
Hugh O'Hara, Garden Manager, Vandeleur Walled Garden, Kilrush, Co Clare
Tel: 087 2240610 (mobile); or Leonard Cleary, Marketing Officer, Kilrush, UDC, Co Clare
Tel: 065 9052891 (mobile)
e-mail: icleary@clarecoco.ie

Nearby sights of interest:
Scattery Island; Cliffs of Moher; the Burren.

Herbaceous borders at Beech Park, County Dublin, focused on a recently installed sundial.

Glossary

allée (French) Meaning literally "a way", this is a path cut through woodland or a shrubbery, or closely flanked by hedges, trees, or walls.

bawn (Irish) An enclosed defended area adjoining or enclosing a castle or manor.

belvedere (Italian) An ornamental building in a commanding position from which a view may be admired.

bosquet (French) A formal grove pierced by sinuous or geometrically arranged walks. Very fashionable between 1670 and 1740. Open spaces, known as *salles* (French), were often incorporated in the layout, sometimes with statues or other ornaments.

bothy (Scots-Irish) Lodgings for garden workers outside a walled garden. In the past bothies varied enormously in the degree of comfort they offered.

Brownian Term used to describe a style of late 18th-century landscape design most often associated with the English landscape designer Lancelot "Capability" Brown (1716–83).

canal An ornamental basin of water, usually rectangular in form.

casita (Spanish) A summer palace, but usually a small house or cottage.

cottage orné (French) Literally, "ornamental cottage". A small rustic building, often thatched, often associated with landscape parks in the *Picturesque* style.

demesne (Norman French) Historically, the lands held by a manor for its own use and occupation, incorporating woods, farmland, parkland, and gardens. The term is still in use in Ireland, though since the break-up of the estate system in the early 20th century its meaning has largely been restricted to landscape parks.

espalier (French) Fruit trees whose branches are pruned and trained into formal patterns against a wall or fence. A wall against which they lean is sometimes also known as an *espalier*.

gazebo (facetious Latin for "I will gaze") A term used to describe a building from which a garden or landscape may be observed.

grotto (Italian) An artificial garden feature made to resemble a natural cave, sometimes adorned with shells.

ha-ha A sunken wall with a ditch, which serves to conceal a boundary and allow uninterrupted views of a landscape to be enjoyed.

Jacobean During the reign of James I (1603–25).

knot An intricate, often interlaced, design, formed by low clipped shrubs such as box, enclosing flowers or decorative gravels.

landscape park An informal ornamental landscape comprising belts of trees bounding open expanses of turf, often decorated with a scatter of isolated trees, clumps, lakes, and garden buildings. Most examples in Ireland date from between 1740 and 1845.

Palladian A style of architecture, popular in Ireland in the 18th century, which was based on classical Roman principles, as reinterpreted by Andrea Palladio, a 16th-century Italian architect.

pagoda (Portuguese/Indian) A building of pyramidal form, usually built in a series of diminishing stages with boldly projecting roofs.

parterre (French) A formal bedding with low hedges, often of box, disposed in a regular way and often incorporating topiary, urns, or other decorative devices. A *parterre de broderie* is a form of parterre in which the hedges are arranged in long, flowing patterns which imitate embroidery patterns.

patte d'oie (French) Literally, a goose foot. A series of usually five alleys or avenues radiating from a central point, especially associated with the gardens of the 17th-century French garden designer André Le Nôtre.

pergola A framework of vertical and horizontal beams, usually over a path, used to form an arch of climbing plants. Very popular in the Edwardian era.

Picturesque school A style of landscape gardening, popular in the late 18th and early 19th centuries, in which beauty implied roughness in texture and ruggedness in delineation.

plat (French) A flat area of mown grass bounded by paths.

potager (French) A kitchen garden, usually of a formal or decorative design.

putti (Italian) Ornamental cherubs, especially associated with Baroque architecture, painting, and gardens.

quincunx (Latin) A geometric planting pattern, usually of trees, comprising the corners of a square and a fifth point in the centre.

Rococo (Italian) Style of architecture made distinct by curved forms and elaborate decoration.

vista (Latin) A long view, usually framed, as in the form of an avenue or a woodland glade.

wilderness A form of *bosquet*, comprising woodland dissected by paths and vistas.

Biographies

Dickson, George (1832–1914) Son of Alexander Dickson, who founded the famous firm of rose breeders Dickson's. He won numerous gold medals for his roses. The firm still flourishes in County Down.

Forrest, George (1873-1932) Scottish plant collector, whose activities were concentrated in Yunnan, Szechuan, Tibet and upper Burma from 1904 until his death (in Yunnan). His numerous new introductions include 300 rhododendrons and over fifty primulas.

Fraser, James (1793–1863) Scottish landscape gardener who worked in Ireland for most of his career. Apart from designing numerous parks and gardens, he was well known as the author of a series of guidebooks.

Henry, Augustine (1857–1930) Ireland's most successful plant collector, he later became Professor of Forestry at the Royal College of Science, Dublin. Most of his plant collecting was in China, and all gardeners are indebted to him for introducing numerous important plants.

Jekyll, Gertrude (1843–1932) English garden designer, artist, and writer who applied her painterly skills to the design possibilities of herbaceous plants. She was strongly influenced by the Arts and Crafts Movement and by *William Robinson*, and advocated a "rational blend" of naturalism and formalism.

King, William (active 1780–1800) Landscape designer who practised in the northern part of Ireland during the late 18th century. He was responsible for the parks at Castle Coole, Mount Stewart, Downhill, and Florence Court, among others.

Kingdon Ward, Frank (1885-1958) The most successful English plant hunter of his generation. His explorations to Yunnan, Szechuan, Assam, Burma and Tibet from 1911 are recorded in a series of twenty books. Quite a number of garden owners in Ireland contributed to his expeditions and consequently many of his new discoveries, such as the yellow flowering *Rhododendron wardii*, are a feature of Irish gardens.

Lutyens, Sir Edwin (1869–1944) English architect and garden designer, who (from 1893 onwards) often worked in conjunction with *Gertrude Jekyll*.

McGredy, Sam (1828–1903) Founder of the famous firm of rose breeders McGredy's, which survived in County Down until the 1970s.

Moore, Sir Frederick (1857–1949) Succeeded his father, David Moore, as the director of the Botanic Gardens at Glasnevin, Dublin, in 1879. He remained director for 43 years, during which time he developed the gardens to a high international standard. He was involved in the evolution of many contemporary Irish gardens.

Niven, Ninian (1799–1879) Scottish-born garden designer, who dominated the field in Ireland during the Victorian era. He specialized in large formal gardens in the French style and worked mostly for the *nouveau riche* rather than the gentry.

Paxton, Sir Joseph (1803–65) English gardener and architect, who is best remembered as the designer of the Crystal Palace, London. He helped to remodel Lismore Castle for the Duke of Devonshire.

Peto, Harold (1854–1933) English architect whose garden designs were strongly influenced by formal Italian gardens, as at Buscot Park (Oxfordshire), Iford Manor (Wiltshire), and Garnish Island (Cork).

Robertson, Daniel (active 1800–1850s) Scottish architect and garden designer who worked in Ireland from 1829 until his death in the 1850s. Much of his known Irish work is in south Leinster. He was, we are told, "given to drink and always drew best when excited with sherry".

Robinson, William (1838–1935) Irish horticulturalist, who had a profound influence on garden taste and design in later Victorian times. He began his career as a garden boy at Curraghmore, County Waterford, but on moving to England he become a highly successful and prosperous garden author. He inveighed against artificiality and advocated suiting the garden to the ground and the plant to the situation.

Ross, Sir John, of Bladensburg One of the great plantsmen of his time, he had a notable garden at Rostrevor, which no longer exists. He advised on the development of many gardens, notably Mount Stewart.

Sutherland, John (c1750–1826) Ireland's premier landscape gardener from the 1780s until the 1820s. He specialized in demesne landscaping but also designed buildings, including glasshouses, and created town parks.

Turner, Richard (c1798–1881) Ironmaster based in Dublin (Hammersmith, Ballsbridge) who became the most successful designer of cast-iron glasshouses in the Victorian age. His many works include the Palm House, Kew (1844–8), and the curvilinear range at Glasnevin, Dublin (1845–6).

Walpole, Edward Horace (1880–1964) Grandson of the founder of Mount Usher gardens and largely responsible for establishing Mount Usher as one of the great gardens of Ireland.

Wilson, Ernest Henry (1876-1930) English plant collector, who travelled extensively in China collecting for Veitch Nurseries between 1898-1905. From 1909 he worked for the Arnold Arboretum near Boston, collecting both in China and Japan. Many of his numerous introductions are found in Irish gardens, notably Annesgrove, Co. Cork, Birr, Co. Offaly, and Rowallane, Co. Down.

Wilson, Guy L (1885–1962) Renowned daffodil grower and breeder from Broughshane, County Antrim. He favoured white varieties, being especially well known for his seedlings of this colour.

Index

Author's Acknowledgements

I was welcomed with courtesy, helpfulness and generous hospitality into numerous gardens and homes in the course of writing this book. I should like to thank in alphabetical order: Tim and Darina Allen; John Anderson; Antrim Borough Council (Michael McLaughlin and John McNeill); Countess Anne Bernstorff; John Bevan; The Hon. David Bigham; John Bourke; Dick and Phyl Boyce; Brian and Noreen Brown; Catherine Burke, Nick Burrowes; Mary Byrne; Kieran and Amabel Clark; Ambrose Congreve; Brian Cross; Helen and Val Dillon; Christine Fehily; Desmond, the Knight of Glin and Madam Olda FitzGerald; Cormac Foley; Paddy Forde; Duncan Forsythe; Knox Gass; David Gilliland and Jennifer Johnson; Anne Golden; Robert and Susan Guinness; Cicely and Robin Hall; Charlie and Ann Hamilton; Mark and Emma Hewlett; Mrs and Mrs Hurley; Harry Hutchman; Trish Hyde; Sir Richard and Lady Olivia Keane; Mary Keenan; Susan Kellett; Jessica Kreissig; Arthur Lardner; James and Elizabeth Leslie; Frances McDonald; Tom McErlean; John Madden; Ester Malony; Nigel Marshall; Helen and Bryan Miller; Nicholas and Susan Mosse; Hugh and Valerie Montgomery; Charles and Emily Naper; Doyne and Georgina Nicholson; Cyril O'Brien; John O'Driscoll; Thomas and Valerie Pakenham; Lady Jessica Rathdonnell; David and Moira Robertson; David Robinson; Peter and Irene Roche; The Earl of Rosse; Martin Sherry and Ken Lambert; Daphne Shackleton; Brigitte Shelswell-White; Sarah Slazenger; George and Michelina Stackpool; Donal Synnott; Bridget Tracey and Denis Shannon; Ursula Walsh; Tim Wallis; Mrs Nesbit Waddington; The Marquess of Waterford and his butler Basil. Thanks to Belinda Jupp for helpfully supplying information on a number of gardens; to my sisters and their families for allowing me to use their homes as bases for garden visiting; Carola and Eric McKeever; Justina and Mark McKeever; Alice Reeves-Smyth and Peter Smith; Anne Reeves-Smyth and Jerry Pullman; and to my mother for all her support at home in County Carlow. At Mitchell-Beazley I would like to thank all those involved in producing the book, in particular Michèle Byam, Selina Mumford, Jenny Faithfull, Terry Hirst and Richard Dawes.

Terence Reeves-Smyth, October 2000

Photographic acknowledgements

All photographs by Terence Reeve-Smyth except the following: back jacket flap Carola McKeever; p.37 Crown Copyright. Reproduced by permission of the Controller of Her Majesty's Stationary Office; p.45 Patrick Quigley; pp. 114–15 OPG/Stephen Robson.